Measuring Clinical Outcome in Stroke

(ACUTE CARE)

Edited by

Anthony Rudd, Michael Pearson and Andrew Georgiou

February 2000

Clinical Effectiveness & Evaluation Unit

ROYAL COLLEGE OF PHYSICIANS

Acknowledgements

The editors wish to acknowledge the major role played by participating pilot sites in the deliberations and assessments contained in this publication. A special thanks must also go to the staff of the Clinical Effectiveness and Evaluation Unit, particularly Barbara Durr, who was important to the production of this document. Finally, we would like to acknowledge the role of the National Centre for Health Outcomes and Development whose collaboration was critical to the success of the work.

Cover illustration: Stipple engraving by G T Stubbs, 1815
Reproduced by kind permission of the Wellcome Institute Library, London

ROYAL COLLEGE OF PHYSICIANS OF LONDON
11 St Andrews Place, London NW1 4LE

Registered Charity No 210508

British Library Cataloguing in Publication Data
A catalogue record for this book is available from the British Library

ISBN 1 86016 121 9

Designed and typeset by the Publications Unit of the Royal College of Physicians

Printed in Great Britain by Sarum Colourview Group, Salisbury, Wiltshire

Contents

CHAPTER 8

A summary of the seminar discussion of stroke outcome indicators
David Barer, Walter W Holland and Derick Wade

APPENDICES

Foreword

Stroke is the commonest cause of adult disability and the third leading cause of death in the UK. It is crucial therefore that effective strategies for the prevention and treatment of stroke are implemented. The last decade has seen important changes in the understanding of the disease, both in terms of the patho-physiology and the systems that need to be implemented to provide effective treatment. In 1989 guidelines published by the Royal College of Physicians for the management of stroke foresaw much of the research evidence that has accumulated since. Its recommendations – that each district should have a physician appointed with a special interest in stroke, and that stroke patients should be managed on special units – have been confirmed and supported by an extensive and rapidly growing body of evidence. Moreover, as the recently published National Sentinel Audit of Stroke has documented, despite considerable progress in the development of stroke services, standards overall remain well below what should be regarded as the acceptable level.

One of the important strategies that is available for improving quality is the development and use of outcome measures that are feasible to collect within a busy clinical service and provide information that enables clinicians and managers locally to identify strengths and weaknesses within their service. For a disease such as stroke, where patients are being provided with care from many different clinicians of different professions, often on several wards within a hospital, the only way of knowing whether care is adequate is by formal measurement of standards. There are potential difficulties in collecting and interpreting such data. Many of the indicators are measures of process rather than clinical outcome. This reflects the difficulty in linking treatment with outcome when detailed and reliable measures of case severity are not available.

The work that has been done by the Clinical Effectiveness and Evaluation Unit in piloting four of the outcome measures has illustrated, that data collection is feasible and can be informative. This work combined with National Audit and National Guidelines for the Management of Stroke, soon to be published by the Royal College of Physicians Intercollegiate Stroke Working Party, provides a comprehensive set of documentation on which Trusts can design, run and monitor an effective, evidence based service. In the age of clinical governance, the measurement of quality of care should become routine. It is both right and proper that clinicians should play a leading role in identifying appropriate measures with which a stroke service should be evaluated.

KGMM ALBERTI
President, Royal College of Physicians

February 2000

Summary

This publication is the product of a project undertaken by the Clinical Effectiveness and Evaluation Unit (CEEU) of the Royal College of Physicians. The aim of the project was to pilot a selection of outcome indicators relating to the care and management of stroke patients in an acute care setting.

The setting:

One of the key themes of the white paper, *The New NHS* is the concept of clinical governance highlighting the responsibility of NHS organisations for the quality of health care. The measurement of outcomes as a means of monitoring and improving health care is critical to this approach.

Outcomes indicators for the NHS:

Health outcomes have been defined as changes in health, health-related status or risk factors affecting health. Indicators are aggregated statistical measures that describe a group of patients or a whole population, compiled from measures or assessments made on people in a group or population. Health outcome indicators can have a number of uses: they can help to monitor progress over time or aid in determining the extent of variation and serve as a 'benchmark' for comparative study.

There are many important reasons why effective indicators of outcome are needed for stroke, it is a major cause of death in the population and is responsible for a large proportion of disability in the population involving a wide range of services and professions throughout the community. The routine information currently available in the NHS is on activity and not effectiveness. Moreover the consistency and quality of the data is limited, making it very difficult to undertake robust analyses. Outcomes of care are not routinely monitored and there is no formal means of assessing the effectiveness of care.

The National Centre for Health Outcomes Development (NCHOD) stroke working group was constituted from a wide range of disciplines involved in the care of stroke patients. It produced a list of 29 outcome indicators for the prevention, treatment and management of stroke patients. Four of those indicators were chosen for the purposes of this study:

- Incidence of pressure sores during the inpatient stay within a hospital provider unit population with a primary diagnosis of stroke.

- Multi-professional involvement in the week following admission within a provider unit population admitted with a primary diagnosis of stroke.

- Distribution of the Barthel Index of Activities of Daily Living (ADL) scores at discharge from hospital, within a provider unit population with a primary diagnosis of stroke.

- Percentage of patients within a provider unit population for whom a formal swallowing assessment was undertaken within 24 hours of a stroke.

A number of important questions underpinned this pilot study. These centred on issues like the feasibility of collecting the data, the standardisation of definitions, and the interpretation of the illustrative data collected from the study, along with the potential for implementing outcome indicators in a way that would be both useful and effective for clinicians, management and patients.

These issues formed the basis of a seminar held at the Royal College of Physicians on 1 July 1998 that brought together professionals from a range of disciplines, including many who had been involved in the pilot study, to discuss the results of the project and provide recommendations for the future of the work. The seminar concluded with agreement that the four pilot indicators were each worth collecting and that if used carefully the data generated from the indicators should help to improve the management of acute stroke care. Two items were recommended for routine collection in every unit (pressure sores and Barthel ADL). The other two items (multi-professional involvement and swallowing assessment) were recommended for periodic collection, eg for a month in every year or two.

The publication of this book will hopefully represent an important step in the development and implementation of health outcome indicators for acute stroke care and the health service in general.

1 Introduction

Anthony Rudd[†] and Michael Pearson[*]

[†]Consultant Physician, St Thomas' Hospital [*]Director, Clinical Effectiveness and Evaluation Unit

The purpose of creating the National Health Service in 1948 was to improve the health of the population of the UK. However progress on this laudable aim has been difficult to evaluate because of the absence of appropriate and reliable measures with which to assess the outcome of healthcare. The NHS collects many statistics, most of which refer to activity within the service rather than to the effectiveness of that activity or quality of the service. This publication describes and discusses clinical outcome measures in acute stroke care with the aim of contributing to the development of health outcome indicators for the NHS.

In 1996 the National Centre for Health Outcomes Development (NCHOD – previously known as the Central Health Outcomes Unit) – set up a series of multidisciplinary working parties to develop and recommend outcome indicators for 10 common conditions: stroke, asthma, fractured neck of femur, urinary incontinence, diabetes, myocardial infarction, breast cancer, severe mental illness, cataract, pregnancy. The Clinical Effectiveness and Evaluation Unit (CEEU) of the Royal College of Physicians has been actively involved in seven of the 10 working groups.

This publication is based upon the presentations and deliberations of a seminar held at the Royal College of Physicians in London in July 1998 that discussed a selection of outcome indicators in acute stroke care. It includes a summation of the seminar's evaluation of the outcome indicators drawn from the concluding presentations of David Barer, Walter Holland and Derick Wade (pp63–73).

The context for the new interest in health outcome measures is discussed by Michael Goldacre (pp7–9). He notes that the expectation that the NHS will become much more outcome driven is based on the recognition that the Department of Health and the NHS presently uses more information about structure (number of beds etc) and process (number of admissions) than it does for outcomes. The concepts of structure, process and outcome are illustrated in Fig 1.

How do we define 'health outcomes' and 'outcome indicators'?

Health outcomes have been defined as changes in health, health-related status, or risk factors affecting health. *Indicators* are aggregated statistical measures that describe a group of patients or a whole population, compiled from measures or assessments made on people in the group or population. They are designed to show up what should and realistically can be known about the outcomes of diseases and health care.

Why stroke?

There are a number of important reasons why stroke should be chosen as one of the first topics for developing effective indicators of outcome. As Charles Wolfe points out in 'The impact of illness' (pp11–20), stroke comprises a group of diseases which are a significant cause of death, adult disability and loss of quality of life. Stroke disease has a major impact on patients and their families, on the health care professionals managing acute and long-term needs, and on the health and social services that plan stroke care. Today stroke is the third highest cause of death and the leading cause of severe disability in the country. Every year, in England and Wales alone, 100,000 people have first strokes. Treatment and care of stroke requires a wide range of services involving different professions within hospital agencies, the community and the patient's home.

The report of the Clinical Standards Advisory Group, *Clinical effectiveness using stroke care as an example*, notes that the consistency and quality of routine information currently available in the NHS is limited and its reliability difficult to measure, and that this is particularly so in the area of stroke care where individuals may be cared for in different settings on many occasions.[2] The report also notes that the outcomes of care are not routinely monitored by NHS Trusts, and even the level of clinical audit of stroke is surprisingly low.

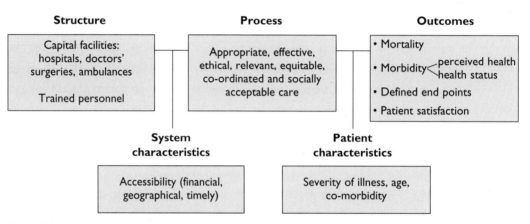

Fig 1. The dimensions of quality care

How were the outcome indicators devised?

The NCHOD working groups produced lists of candidate indicators that aimed to be:

- Reliable, relevant and useful to everyday care
- Valid and responsive to changes in health
- Research-based, linking effective processes of care and patient outcomes

The working groups recommended indicators according to their potential role in:

- reducing risk of attack
- early detection of disease
- assuring return to function
- reducing adverse impact on well-being
- reducing risk of death

They were asked additionally to bear in mind a number of potential uses for outcome information:

- For clinical decision-making and audit of clinical work, including the management of patients; management of health professionals' practice; audit of health professionals' practice and research.

- For informing decisions about strategic and operational development of services.

- For comparisons of the organisations involved in the delivery of service. Such comparisons can be either provider, purchaser, or population-based.

- For assessing progress towards standards or targets for health outcomes, agreed locally or nationally, which may be identified from research literature or set by clinical and managerial decisions.

The CEEU has been centrally involved in piloting a selection of the clinical indicators devised by the various working groups with the aim of assessing such issues as:

Feasibility — What is the method of data collection? What is the quality of data? Who collects the data? Are the data complete?

Standardisation — Testing the standardisation of the definitions used. The degree of generalisation: what is the level of comparability across different conditions, populations and different types of investigations?

Illustrative values — Producing illustrative values and assessing the extent of variation.

Interpretation — What are the indicator values telling us? Are they robust/reliable/relevant? Does the indicator actually measure what it is intended to measure?

In the area of stroke, four outcome indicators were selected for piloting (see Appendix: Candidate indicators, pp75–83 for a detailed description of the candidate indicators). The indicators as listed below are related to the care and management of stroke patients with a primary diagnosis of stroke in an acute setting:

1   Incidence of pressure sores during the inpatient stay within a hospital provider unit population.

2   Multi-professional involvement in the week following admission.

3   Distribution of the Barthel Index of Activities of Daily Living (ADL), at discharge from hospital.

4   Percentage of patients for whom a formal swallowing assessment was undertaken within 24 hours of a stroke.

The pilot project utilised the Royal College of Physicians Minimum Data Set (MDS),[3] itself the product of an intercollegiate, multidisciplinary working group, as described in the presentation by Penny Irwin in pp25–28. The minimum data set concept provides a simple and straightforward way of gathering key data with which to enable comparison and evaluation. The choice of items for the data set was the result of a vigorous process which drew on the best research evidence available. The items included relate to casemix, process and outcome and were selected on the criteria that they were: i) specific to stroke, ii) predictive of outcome; and iii) constitute discreet indicators that are easy to collect.

Understanding and using outcome indicators

The problems of achieving reliable and valid outcome indicators are examined in the presentation by Anthony Rudd (pp21–24). There are many unanswered questions about stroke, along with some important, but still unclarified, epidemiological issues. For instance, there is still great difficulty in reaching consensus about the definition of casemix measures, such as age, gender and disease variation. Consideration also needs to be given to the impact of environment on the management of stroke, for example, quality of housing and care settings. In some cases, pure outcome measures are very difficult to devise and it is more worthwhile to use process measures as proxy outcome indicators.

A public health perspective

There are many methodological issues involved in the measurement of health outcomes which should be recognised and anticipated. Measuring outcomes is not just concerned with the collection of data but requires consideration of why outcomes are to be assessed, along with due attention to the appropriate measures to be used and the choice of a suitable study design.

Jonathan Mant's presentation (pp29–34) deals with many of these issues. He points out that outcome indicators need to be relevant and important to health professionals and managers. Variations in outcome measures need to be understood, and the differences need to be evaluated for what they are saying. It is also crucial to consider the cost of collecting the data and ensuring its completeness, accuracy and standardisation. And finally, it is necessary to consider who will be using the data, eg patients, health care professionals, management, primary care groups, patients etc.

The pilot study

Andrew Georgiou outlines the methodology and results of a project undertaken by the CEEU to pilot the chosen indicators (pp35–62). The study found different levels of swallowing assessment and incidence of pressure sores among the pilot sites. The dependency of patients using the Barthel Activities of Daily Living (ADL) Functional Assessment Scale was measured and differences in the data collection process and the quality of data were also identified. The study drew attention to critical issues such as the need for precisely defined variables to eliminate alternative interpretations and ensure standardised and comparable data, available to those who require it, when and where it is needed.

The pilot study report has been supplemented by accounts by a selection of participating pilot sites who have documented, analysed and discussed their own studies. Their comments provide valuable insights and observations based on the experience of actually collecting and using data. This helped to inform the seminar's 'evaluation of the indicators' designated aims, rationale and potential uses.

The seminar concluded with agreement that the four pilot indicators were worth collecting and could help to improve stroke management. Two items were recommended for routine collection in every unit (pressure sores and Barthel Assessment of Daily Living). The other two items were recommended for periodic collection: eg one month every one to two years (multi-professional involvement and swallowing assessment). The seminar also agreed that a measure of patient well-being should be part of (routine) data collection.

We are confident that the work described in this document marks an important step towards measuring outcome measures for stroke that are relevant to patients, clinicians and managers. The next step is to incorporate outcome indicators into NHS information systems so that they can become useful and effective tools for improving health care.

References

1. Mayor S. *How to reduce your risk of stroke*. London: Stroke Association, 1997.

2. Clinical Standards Advisory Group. *Report on clinical effectiveness using stroke care as an example*. London: The Stationary Office, 1998.

3. Irwin P, Rudd A. Casemix and process indicators of outcome in stroke. *J R Coll Physicians Lond* 1998; **32**: 442–4.

2 Developing health outcome indicators: an overview

Michael Goldacre

Director, Unit of Healthcare Epidemiology, University of Oxford

Background

At present, in assessing the provision of medical care, the National Health Service currently makes more use of information about structure (eg number of beds, equipment etc) and process (eg, number of admissions, lengths of stay) than it does about outcomes. By and large, outcome indicators are not generally available, but there is an increasing expectation that the NHS will become more outcome-driven, as confirmed by the 1997 White Paper, *The New NHS*,[1] and the government's consultation document, *A first class service: quality in the new NHS*.[2] The Department of Health recognises that existing outcome indicators have been developed using routinely available data collected for purposes other than measuring health outcomes (eg data from death certificates that are collected fundamentally for legal reasons). Health outcome indicators derived from current routine data have therefore tended to be compiled opportunistically rather than with the objective of what ideally we would wish to know about the outcomes of care.

The Department of Health commissioned work on developing outcome indicators for ten clinical conditions, beginning with asthma, and stroke. Groups were established to debate and formulate recommendations for each of the chosen conditions. Membership was broadly based, and comprised physicians and other health professionals, and included representatives of management, research bodies and patients' interests. The groups drew on the services of CASPE Research for their knowledge of information systems, and on the UK Clearing House on Health Outcomes for their expertise on health outcome measurement instruments. The York Centre for Reviews and Dissemination assisted in compiling systematic reviews.

To respond to criticism about the paucity of work on outcomes the Department of Health threw out a general challenge to the groups and provided a specific remit to make recommendations for 'ideal' indicators of health outcome for each clinical condition. To do this the groups were required to devise methods of working and definitions, starting with the fundamentals such as what is meant by 'ideal indicators of health outcome' (see p8).

The aim of the collaboration was to develop a comprehensive menu of indicators covering what could be assessed in aggregate form in routine practice. In doing so, many more recommendations for indicators were put forward than the NHS would routinely wish, or be able to implement on a routine on-going basis. However, this menu of indicators will hopefully help to guide people in choosing indicators of relevance to their interests as and when they became interested in particular aspects of the measurement of stroke or other clinical conditions. The working groups were keen to emphasise the importance of comparative data for monitoring trends over time, comparing different sites, and in enabling the service to pool and share data from different projects in different parts of the country. It was envisaged that national databases of outcome measures and indicator values could be developed, which could be used as benchmarks against which, for example, hospitals could compare their own local data.

Defining ideal indicators of health outcome

Health outcome was defined as ***change – or lack of change when change is expected – in health, health-related status, or risk factors affecting health***. A central consideration in this work was that outcomes may be attributable to medical interventions or they may be the result of the natural history of the condition. Considerations of casemix, bias and confounding are central to the appropriate interpretation of indicator values.

An indicator was defined as ***an aggregated statistical measure, describing a group or whole population, compiled from measures on individuals, which provides insights about the functioning of services***. Indicators will not necessarily provide definitive answers on whether services are good, adequate or inadequate but, when well chosen, they should be capable of providing *pointers* as to where further investigation may be worthwhile.

Ideal indicators are defined as ***what should be known, and realistically could be known, about outcomes relevant to the condition of interest***.

Finally, the Department of Health encouraged the working groups to think strategically about the situation five years ahead, in recognition that what may not be feasible at present, may well become so in the foreseeable future, particularly with the development of clinical and management information systems. Proposals put forward on outcome indicators may themselves help influence developments in management thinking and developments in medical information technology.

Designing a healthcare model

For each clinical condition, a model was developed to help the working group identify potential indicators. The model included:

- an overview of the epidemiology of the disease, including what is known about its causes and risk factors;
- the course and consequences of the condition;
- relevant interventions.

There was consideration of indicators intended to identify success in:

- reducing the risk of the condition;
- detecting the condition early;
- assuring return to function after an acute episode;
- reducing risk of a further acute episode;

> reducing adverse impact on well-being;

> reducing risk of death.

This model was used to guide the thinking of the working groups to ensure that they had considered outcomes relevant to all important aspects of the condition.

Specification of indicators and recommendations for their use

A detailed specification was developed for each indicator which included: definitions of the condition and the measures to be used; specification of the expected users and uses of each indicator; data sources; potential confounders; and comments about further work which may be required to develop or evaluate the indicator. The working groups made a recommendation about the indicators for each condition, grouping them into the categories of those which:

> should be generally available as a routine;

> should be available, where the means to produce them exist locally, or where their production will be possible after expected developments in information technology, or where there is particular local interest in the topic;

> need further work on either the technical specification, the feasibility of data collection, or the usefulness of the indicator, before definite recommendations could be made.

The working groups also made recommendations about whether the data for each indicator should be collected on a sample basis, and perhaps only periodically, or whether the data should be collected on all relevant patients as an ongoing routine.

There were some indicators — a fairly small number for almost all the conditions — where it was recommended that compilation be carried out on a universal basis as a routine, eg population-based mortality rates for stroke. For others, the recommendation was that when the data were collected as part of periodic reviews, or in *ad hoc* studies or audits, the recommended definitions and specifications should be followed in order to facilitate comparisons with others. Also included was a category of recommendation for further work needed, either because the indicator specification or method of measurement was insufficiently worked up, or because the indicator was thought to be a good idea, but there was insufficient confidence about its utility until it was tested.

This work was undertaken before the White Paper, *The New NHS*,[1] and before the government's proposals on quality initiatives and clinical governance, but it is now clear that the NHS is expected to develop a focus on the assessment of outcomes and quality of care.

References

1. Department of Health. *The new NHS – modern, dependable: a national framework for assessing performance*. London: HMSO, 1997.

2. Department of Health. *A first class service: quality in the new NHS*. London: HMSO, 1998.

3   Stroke: the impact of illness

Charles D A Wolfe

Reader in Public Health Medicine, Guy's, King's and St Thomas' Hospitals School of Medicine, London

This chapter will summarise the impact of stroke, a disease of major socio-economic impact throughout the world, from several perspectives including those of patients, their families and carers, primary care, acute hospitals and commissioners of healthcare, along with policy makers.

The disease

The definition of stroke used in assessing its impact will be that used by the World Health Organization:

> A syndrome of rapidly developing clinical signs of focal (or global) disturbance of cerebral function, with symptoms lasting 24 hours or longer, or leading to death, with no apparent cause other than of vascular origin.

This definition includes subarachnoid haemorrhage but excludes transient ischaemic attack (TIA), subdural haematoma, and haemorrhage or infarction caused by infection or tumour. It also excludes silent cerebral infarct. It would appear that studies are likely to underestimate the total burden of cerebrovascular disease, the data discussed being mainly based on symptomatic strokes.[1]

There are a number of classifications of stroke, none of which is ideal. Routine NHS data utilise the International Classification of Disease (ICD).[2,3] A useful clinically based classification has been developed by Bamford[4] in which prognosis is related to subtype of stroke.

Population based data

. . . useful predominantly for policy makers and purchasers of healthcare although incidence data may be useful for hospitals in planning acute stroke services.

Mortality

Stroke accounts for 10–12% of all deaths in industrialised countries; 88% of victims are over the age of 65. In 1997 there were 57,747 deaths in England and Wales from stroke, with 2,525 from subarachnoid haemorrhage.[2] Stroke is the third most common cause of death in the UK after myocardial infarction and cancer,[2] and is consequently a focus of attention for the government.

There are noticeable differences in the standardised mortality ratios (SMR) for stroke (ie mortality rates adjusted for age and sex differences in populations) between regions in the UK: 132 (Northumberland) to 75 (NW Hertfordshire) (national SMR=100).[5,6] A study of case-fatality from stroke in southern England did, however, demonstrate that the variation in the

SMR for stroke in three health authorities was due to variations in incidence rather than case-fatality.[6]

In England and Wales during 1993/4, an average of 28 years of life was lost per 10,000 population as a result of stroke. This varied from 21.6 in the South and West region to 34.9 in the North West region.[5]

There has been a significant decrease in mortality from stroke over time. In the western world this started in the early 1900s and has accelerated in the past 30 years. It has been attributed by some to better control of hypertension, although this is far from clear.[5]

Incidence of stroke

. . . defined as the number of first-in-a-lifetime strokes occurring per unit time

Subarachnoid haemorrhage (SAH)

The incidence is about 9–14 per 100,000 per year.[8] Other published estimates are as high as 33 per 100,000 per year in men and 25 per 100,000 per year in women.[9,10] The case-fatality rate is high, 46% within 30 days and 48% at one year.[9,11]

Stroke

There have been many population based studies of stroke, most of which had significant methodological flaws.[11–14] Although the Oxford Community Stroke Project (OCSP) is the gold standard for incidence studies in the UK, it commenced over 15 years ago when mortality rates were higher and the study area was predominantly in rural Oxfordshire with no ethnic minority groups. The overall crude incidence of first-in-a-lifetime stroke was 2.4 per 1,000 per year in Oxford. The recent south London register reports an overall crude incidence rate of 1.3 per 1,000 population, with a 2.2-fold increased risk in the black population.[15] Sudlow & Warlow estimated that internationally in the age group 45–84, incidence rates ranged from 3 to 5 per 1,000.[16]

The incidence of all acute strokes (first and recurrent) is in the region of 20-30% higher than the first-in-a-lifetime rate[17,18] although there are no recent UK data to draw upon.

Subtypes of stroke

Intracerebral haemorrhage (excluding SAH) accounts for just over 10% of all strokes, the remainder being due to cerebral infarction.[14] Lacunar stroke syndrome constitutes about 21% of first strokes, and has a crude annual incidence of 0.33 per 1,000.[19] These stroke patients have a much lower case-fatality rate (10% at one year), and 66% are functionally independent at 1 year. Using the Bamford classification, the following proportions of causes of first strokes can be expected:[11] cerebral infarction 76% (partial anterior circulation 56%, lacunar 20%, total anterior circulation 15%, posterior circulation 8%, unclassified 1%); primary intracerebral haemorrhage 10%; subarachnoid haemorrhage 4%; not known 10%.

Bonita[20] has estimated that the risk of a person of 45 years of age having a stroke within 20 years is very low (about 1 in 30). However, almost 1 in 4 men and nearly 1 in 5 women aged 45 can expect to have a stroke if they live to their 85th year. Although the lifetime risk of having an acute stroke is higher in men than women, the converse is true for the lifetime risk of dying of a stroke. Thus about 16% of all women are likely to die of a stroke compared with 8% of men; this difference is largely attributable to the higher mean age at stroke onset in women, and to their greater life expectancy. Typically, first events account for about 75% of all acute events. The cumulative risk of recurrence over 5 years is high, ranging from about a third to almost a half of people who have a stroke.

Trends in stroke incidence and case-fatality

. . . useful data for health care planners and acute hospitals

Incidence

There have been few stroke incidence registers that have been maintained over long enough periods of time to document a change in incidence. Moreover, the results from these registers are contradictory. Since stroke rates increase greatly with age, and the number of elderly people is increasing, the burden of stroke on individual families and on the health services is unlikely to fall rapidly. Malmgren[21] estimated that between 1983 and 2023 there will be an absolute increase in the number of patients experiencing a first-ever stroke of about 30%. There will be an increase in the number of deaths from stroke of about 40%, and there will only be an increase of 4–8% in the number of disabled long-term survivors. There can be an anticipated increase in the need for acute care and early rehabilitation services over this time period, but not in longer-term care.

Case-fatality

Case-fatality measures the proportion of people who die within a specified period after the stroke; comparisons are based on the first-ever stroke in a lifetime since recurrent strokes have a higher case-fatality. One-month case-fatality rates are dependent on the age structure and health status of the populations studied; they vary from 17% to 49% amongst men in the MONICA studies and 18% to 57% in women,[22] with an average of about 24% from the literature. In the UK the OCSP 28-day case-fatality was 19% overall; that for cerebral infarction was 10%, primary intracerebral haemorrhage 50%, and subarachnoid haemorrhage 46%.[11] About half the deaths within the first month are due to the direct neurological sequelae of the stroke.[11] After 30 days non-stroke cardiovascular disease becomes increasingly important and is the most common cause of death after the first year.[23] The 1-year case-fatality rate in the OCSP study was 31% but with marked differences between subtypes: cerebral infarction 23%; primary intracerebral haemorrhage 62%; subarachnoid haemorrhage 48%. The most important prognostic factors for survival are unfortunately not currently amenable to health service intervention (retention of consciousness, younger age, no history of stroke, urinary incontinence).[6,24]

In the OCSP study the five-year survival rate was 55%, which compares with 52% (male) and 60% (female) in the Framingham study, USA, 46% in Rochester, 28% in Moscow and 39% in Ikawa.[23,25–28] Predictably, older patients have a worse absolute survival but, relative to the general population, stroke also increased the relative risk of dying in younger patients. After the first month of suffering a stroke, cardiovascular disease becomes the most common cause of death after the first year.[23]

Data on trends in case-fatality rates based on epidemiological studies are scarce. A reduction of 50% in the 30-day case-fatality following stroke from 33% to 17% was observed in the Rochester study during the periods 1945–49 and 1980–84.[29] Since some of the improvements in case-fatality occurred during the time when incidence was declining, increased detection of milder cases is unlikely to be the only reason for the observed changes. In the Soderhamn study, 3-year survival improved by 15.4% and 5.5% for men and women, respectively, between the two study periods 1975–78 and 1983–87; there was no difference in 30-day survival. Most of the long-term improvement occurred between 2 and 6 months after the stroke and was attributed to fewer fatal complications rather than a reduced risk of recurrent stroke.[30] In New Zealand the overall 28-day case-fatality declined from 27.1% to 21.9% in men and from 37.6% to 25.8% in women from 1981 to 1991, but the decline was not statistically significant in any age or sex group.[31]

Prevalence of stroke

. . . useful for health care planners and primary care

The prevalence of stroke is the number of stroke sufferers in the population. There have been very few prevalence surveys of stroke, the prevalence rates being estimated using the incidence and survival data from stroke registers. O'Mahony[32] and colleagues validated a simple self-completed questionnaire to screen for cases of stroke in the community; they estimated that 10% of respondents reported a history of stroke, and the question 'Have you ever had a stroke?' had a sensitivity of 95% and a specificity of 96%.

There have been estimates of the prevalence of stroke, such as in Australia where it was estimated that there are 5–8 stroke sufferers per 1,000 population over the age of 25 years.[33] It was estimated that about 50% of prevalent survivors could use public transport unaided. Aho[34] estimated the prevalence of stroke in a Finnish population in the 1970s. The overall prevalence rate was 6.4 per 1,000 (men 7.9, women 4.8). Of the 87% assessed for disability, 24% had no significant disability, 33% only slight disability, 28% moderate disability, and 16% more severe disability. Overall, about 44% had difficulties with walking. A study in Copenhagen estimated the prevalence to be 5.18 per 1,000 persons,[35,36] and estimated a total prevalence rate of 46.8 (95% confidence intervals 42.5–51.6) per 10,000 population.

Defining impairment, disability and handicap

. . . useful to health care planners, acute hospitals, primary care, patients and families using World Health Organization definitions[37]

Impairment refers to abnormalities arising at the level of the organism. Impairments are usually the external manifestations of the pathology: the symptom and signs (outlined in Table 1). Impairments are 'objective' and cover a wide range of states that carry no personal meaning to the patient: hemianopia, sensory loss, muscle weakness, spasticity, pain etc. Some medical and surgical treatments aim to reduce these impairments.

Table 1. Acute (0–7 days), three-week and six-month impairment/disability dependency rates.[38]

Phenomenon	Acute %	3 weeks %	6 months %
Impairments			
Initial loss/depression of consciousness	5	–	–
Not oriented (or unable to talk)	55	36	27
Marked communication problems (aphasia)	52	29	15
Motor loss (partial or complete)	80	70	53
Disabilities			
Incontinent of faeces	31	13	7
Incontinent of urine	44	24	11
Needs help grooming (teeth, face, hair)	56	27	13
Needs help with toilet/commode	68	39	20
Needs help with feeding	68	38	33
Needs help moving from bed to chair	70	42	19
Unable to walk independently indoors	73	40	15
Needs help dressing	79	51	31
Needs help bathing	86	65	49
Dependency			
Very severely dependent	38	13	4
Severely dependent	20	13	5
Moderately dependent	15	15	12
Mildly dependent	12	28	32
Physically independent	12	31	47

Note: The 'acute' figures are of limited accuracy as many patients were not assessed within the first week; many of these were very ill and probably very dependent. Consequently, the figures relating to acute disability are minimum estimates. These data relate only to survivors.

Disability refers to changes in the interactions between the patient and the environment. It is the behavioural consequences, that manifest within the patient's environment, or the personally meaningful functions or activities that are no longer executed or are altered. Altered behaviours stretch from continence and turning over in bed to dressing, bathing and gardening, interacting with other people, and specific work skills. In practical terms, especially in relation to health and social services, disability manifests itself as an increasing dependence upon people and/or environmental adaptations.

Some representative data on disability for the acute phase and six months are shown in Table 1, taken from Wade[38] using mainly UK data.[39-43] The OCSP study has estimated the disability levels at one year. Sixty-five percent (95% confidence intervals 61–69%) of survivors were functionally independent, which varied by subtype: cerebral infarction 65% (95% CI 60–70%), intracerebral haemorrhage 68% (95% CI 50–86%), and subarachnoid haemorrhage 76% (95% CI 56–96%). Owing to the small numbers involved, these estimates are not robust. Martin[44] estimated that stroke was the most common cause of adult disability in the UK.

Handicap is the most difficult level to define and measure; it is the change in social position that arises from illness, and also refers to the social, societal and personal consequences of the disease. It is the roles and expectations that are performed less readily, if at all.

Longer-term outcome

The longer-term outcome of stroke is not well defined; it has been difficult to assess the longer-term effect of stroke since age and concurrent illnesses also affect outcome assessment. In a survey in south London, the vast majority of stroke survivors, five years after their stroke, lived in private accommodation, and the most disabled were likely to be in private accommodation only if they had an identified carer.[45] One-third of survivors were severely or moderately disabled and two-fifths of survivors were more disabled than they had been at three months after their stroke. Respite care was received by only a few people. Nearly 75% had an adaptation to the environment and 75% were prescribed treatments aimed at preventing further vascular events. Twenty three per cent were depressed and a further 14% had borderline depression scores. The assessment of quality of life suggested that the patient scores on the various scales were related to their residual disability.

Needs of families and carers

In recent years there has been an increasing, but unproven, emphasis on the need for stroke services managed in the community. The strategists and health service planners have not taken account of the considerable proportion of care undertaken by carers and families. As a result of the pressures, carers may suffer from depression and anxiety. Family tensions and financial problems are common. Four main areas of concern to carers can be identified through the literature. Carers want information, skills training, emotional support and regular respite. However, these have been highlighted as areas of major deficiency in informal carers' interactions with professionals. Carers frequently mentioned a failure of agencies to supply promised aids or services, a general lack of information and advice, and the provision of irrelevant help. These points obviously have great implications for the type of help offered to carers. The nursing literature does suggest the importance of nurses in information giving and counselling: 'the support of informal carers must be seen as a legitimate and important focus for nursing interventions.' Yet the literature also highlights the fact that, on the whole, this has not been happening. The literature also cites the benefits of intervention, such as that of support groups for patients and their carers. However, it has also been shown that these may benefit only certain people, and there is a lack of proper evaluation of such groups.[46]

Current service provision for stroke

It was estimated many years ago that stroke services accounted for at least 4% of the NHS budget, but that figure did not take into account social services and carer costs.

Primary care

Stroke is estimated to account for 7% of emergency calls seen out-of-hours.[47] The morbidity survey in general practice[48] estimates that circulatory diseases account for 9% of consultations, 36% of which are 'serious', the most common reason being for essential hypertension. Overall cerebrovascular disease prevalence was estimated at 5–8 per 1,000 individuals. Nearly all patients who consulted for cerebrovascular disease did so for transient cerebral ischaemia or for acute but ill-defined cerebrovascular disease. Comparison of prevalence rates for 1971/2 and 1991/2 shows an overall 64% increase in consultation rates. The number of contacts for follow-up of a stroke would appear from the statistics to be low.

There have been audits of services received by patients discharged from stroke units, but these are biased as they do not detail the resources available or consumed by non-admitted patients. Ebrahim[49] audited services 6 months after discharge from hospital. Eighty four per cent of the survivors were at home. Of those interviewed, just over half had seen their GP, 30% a district nurse, 25% a home help and 21% meals-on-wheels. Outpatient therapy had been received by 42%, most of them disabled patients. Barer[50] contacted district nurse services in Nottingham-shire and identified 369 patients in the community receiving help from the district nursing services. He estimated that only 20% of the expected prevalent cases of severely disabled stroke patients were receiving nursing assistance. In Bristol, Legh-Smith[51] assessed 436 patients one year after their stroke; 88% were at home. The GP had been to see them recently in 44% of cases, the district nurse had visited 19%, 15% were attending a day centre or day hospital, and meals-on-wheels served 8%. Services appeared to be reaching all those that required them.

Secondary health care

Secondary care services for stroke management span many specialties (care of the elderly, acute medicine, neurology, neurosurgery, rehabilitation); the patterns of care vary considerably around the country, depending on a variety of local influences such as historic patterns of care, priority of purchasers and providers to modify traditional service provision, and local enthusiasm and expertise in the management of stroke patients. The balance of care between the different professional groups involved in the management of the stroke patients varies considerably, as does the philosophy of care (therapists, nurses, medical practitioners, psychologists).

Although stroke care usually involves hospitalisation, wide variations have been reported between English districts in the proportion of stroke cases admitted to inpatient care: the hospitalisation rate. A study in Oxford estimated a hospitalisation rate of 55%,[52] and a study of three health authorities in southern England, West Lambeth, Lewisham and North Southwark (both inner-city), Tunbridge Wells (rural), found an overall rate of 71%, with no significant difference between districts.[53] It is impossible to accurately assess hospitalisation rates without the use of registers such as those established in Oxford and southern England. These were introduced for research purposes and their results may not be typical. In his 'needs assessment for stroke' Wade estimated that hospitalisation rates currently vary between health authorities, from 50% to 90%.[38] He went on to argue that, although it is the less severe stroke cases who tend to remain at home, this is not always the case. The implication appears to be that the variation in hospitalisation rates that exist across the country are to a large extent due to variations in local practice and the availability of resources rather than due to variations in casemix.

Routine Hospital Episode Statistics (HES) data can be used to estimate the overall number of admissions for stroke, but these data do not distinguish first from recurrent stroke, and no data are available on the non-admitted patients. It is also impossible to establish with certainty the reason for admission or the validity of the ICD code assigned to the patient, so it is wisest to consider all stroke admissions, with the possible exception of subarachnoid haemorrhage, as one group.[5] HES data for 1994/5 indicate that in England and Wales there were around 2,700 inpatient admissions for subarachnoid haemorrhage and around 67,000 for other types of stroke. It would therefore appear that a larger proportion of patients with a subarachnoid haemorrhage are admitted relative to the overall incidence of stroke subtypes.

It is estimated that in terms of acute stroke services patients consume the following resources: 20% of acute beds; 25% of all long-term beds, including nursing home places.[38] In the Stroke Association survey, 67% of physicians indicated that they routinely cared for patients with acute stroke and around 40% of patients were treated by geriatricians.[54] Few (5%) had access to an acute stroke unit, and a majority (51%) of consultants were uncertain of the benefits of such units. Less than half (44%) had access to a specialised stroke rehabilitation unit, although a majority (68%) were certain of the benefits of stroke rehabilitation units. About one-third of all UK stroke patients were admitted to a hospital without on-site computed tomography (CT) facilities. There are few studies on institutional care and stroke. Barer surveyed nursing homes in Nottingham and estimated that a quarter of beds were occupied by stroke patients and that these patients had a high level of emotional distress and felt lonely.[50,55]

Conclusion

Stroke is a group of diseases which are a significant cause of death, adult disability and loss of quality of life. The disease has profound effects on the patients and their families, the healthcare professionals managing their acute and longer-term needs, and the health and social services planning stroke care.

References

1. Hatona S. Experience from a multicenter stroke register: a preliminary report. *Bull WHO* 1976; **54**: 541–3.

2. Office of National Statistics. Series DH, 2 no.24. *Mortality statistics: causes. England and Wales 1997.* London: HMSO, 1998.

3. Department of Health. *Public Health Common Data Set 1995.* Guildford: Institute of Public Health, University of Surrey, 1996.

4. Bamford J, Sandercock P, Dennis M, Warlow C. Classification and natural history of clinically identifiable subtypes of cerebral infarction. *Lancet* 1991; **337**: 1521–6.

5. Department of Health. *Hospital Episode Statistics,* Vols 1 and 2. England: Financial year 1994-95. Leeds: DoH, 1996.

6. Wolfe CDA, Taub NA, Woodrow J, Richardson E *et al.* Does the incidence severity or case fatality of stroke vary in southern England? *J Epidemiol Community Health* 1993; **47**: 139–43.

7. Department of Health. *Our healthier nation: a contract for health.* London: HMSO, 1998.

8. Sandercock PAG. *The Oxfordshire Community Stroke Project and its application to stroke prevention.* MD Thesis, University of Oxford, 1984.

9. Sarti C, Tuomilehto J, Salomaa V, Sivenius J *et al.* Epidemiology of subarachnoid haemorrhage in Finland from 1983 to 1985. *Stroke* 1991; **22**: 848–53.

10. Bonita R, Thompson S. Subarachnoid haemorrhage: epidemiology, diagnosis, management and outcome. *Stroke* 1985; **16**: 591–4.

11. Bamford J, Sandercock, Dennis M, Burn J *et al*. A prospective study of acute cerebrovascular disease in the community: the Oxfordshire Community Stroke Project. 2. Incidence, case fatality rates and overall outcome at one year of cerebral infarction, primary intracerebral and subarachnoid haemorrhage. *J Neurol Neurosurg Psychiatry* 1990; **53**: 16–22.

12. Malmgren R, Bamford J, Warlow C, Sandercock P. Geographical and secular trends in stroke incidence. *Lancet* 1987; **ii**: 1196–2000.

13. Oxfordshire Community Stroke Project. Incidence of stroke in Oxfordshire: first year's experience of a community stroke register. *Br Med J* 1983; **287**: 713–7.

14. Bamford J, Sandercock P, Dennis M, Warlow C *et al*. A prospective study of acute cerebrovascular disease in the community: the Oxfordshire Community Stroke Project. 1. Methodology, demography and incident cases of first-ever stroke. *J Neurol Neurosurg Psychiatry* 1988; **51**: 1373–80.

15. Stewart JA, Dundas RM, Howant RS, Rudd AP *et al*. Ethnic differences in stroke incidence; a prospective study using a stroke register. *Br Med J* 1999; **318**: 967–71.

16. Sudlow CLM, Warlow CP. Comparable studies of the incidence of stroke and its pathological types: results from the International Stroke Incidence Collaboration *Stroke*. 1997: **28**: 491–9.

17. Herman B, Leyten ACM, Van Luijk JH, Frenken CWGM *et al*. Epidemiology of stroke in Tilburg, The Netherlands. The population-based stroke incidence register: 2. Incidence, initial clinical picture and medical care, and three-week case fatality. *Stroke* 1982; **13**: 629–34.

18. Bonita R, Beaglehole R, North JDK. Event, incidence and case fatality rates of cerebrovascular disease in Auckland, New Zealand. *Am J Epidemiol* 1984; **120**: 236–43.

19. Bamford J, Sandercock P, Jones L, Warlow C. The natural history of lacunar infarction: the Oxfordshire Community Stroke Project. *Stroke* 1987; **18**: 545–51.

20. Bonita R. Epidemiology of stroke. *Lancet* 1992; **339**: 342–4.

21. Malmgren R, Bamford J, Warlow C, Sandercock P *et al*. Projecting the number of patients with first-ever strokes and patients newly handicapped by stroke in England and Wales. *Br Med J* 1989; **298**: 656–60.

22. Thorvaldsen P, Asplund K, Kuutasmaa K, Rajaknagas AM *et al*. Stroke incidence, case fatality, and mortality in the WHO MONICA Project. *Stroke* 1995; **26**: 361–7.

23. Dennis MS, Burn JPS, Sandercock AG, Bamford JM *et al*. Long-term survival after first-ever stroke: the Oxfordshire Community Stroke Project. *Stroke* 1993; **24**: 796–800.

24. Bonita R, Ford M, Stewart AW. Predicting survival after stroke: a three-year follow-up. *Stroke* 1988; **19**: 669–73.

25. Sacco RL, Wolf PA, Kannel WB, McNamara PM. Survival and recurrence following stroke: the Framingham Study. *Stroke* 1982; **13**: 290–5.

26. Dyken ML. Natural history of ischaemic stroke in cerebrovascular disease. In: Harrison MJG, Dyken ML (eds). Butterworth International Medical Reviews. *Neurology* 3rd edn, London: Butterworth, 1983, 139–70.

27. Scmidt EV, Smirnov VE, Ryabova VS. Results of the seven-year prospective study of stroke patients. *Stroke* 1988; **19**: 942–9.

28. Kojima S, Omura T, Wakamatsu W, Kishi M *et al*. Prognosis and disability of stroke patients after 5 years in Akita, Japan. *Stroke* 1990; **21**: 72–7.

29. Garraway W, Whisnant J, Drury I. The continuing decline in the incidence of stroke. *Mayo Clin Proc* 1983; **58**: 520–3.

30. Terent A. Survival after stroke and transient ischaemic attacks during the 1970s and 1980s. *Stroke* 1989; **20**: 1320–6.

31. Bonita R, Broad JB, Beaglehole R. Changes in stroke incidence and case-fatality in Auckland, New Zealand, 1981–91. *Lancet* 1993; **342**: 1470–3.

32. O'Mahony PG, Dobson R, Rodgers H, James OFW *et al.* Validation of a population screening questionnaire to assess prevalence of stroke. *Stroke* 1995; **26**: 1334–7.

33. Christie D. Prevalence of stroke and its sequelae. *Med J Aust* 1981; **2**: 182–4.

34. Aho K, Reunanen A, Aromaa A, Knekt P *et al.* Prevalence of stroke in Finland. *Stroke* 1986; **17**: 681–6.

35. Sorensen PS, Boysen G, Jensen G, Schnohr P. Prevalence of stroke in a district of Copenhagen: the Copenhagen City Heart Study. *Acta Neurol Scand* 1982; **66**: 68–81.

36. Hillman M, Geddes JML, Tennant A, Chamberlain MA. Benefits and services: Stroke survivors living in the community. Stroke Association Annual Scientific Conference, London, 1995.

37. World Health Organization. *The international classification of impairments, disabilities and handicaps.* Geneva, WHO: 1980.

38. Wade D. Stroke (acute cerebrovascular disease). In: Stevens A, Raftery J, (eds). *Health care needs assessments reviews.* Oxford: Radcliffe Medical Press, 1994.

39. Wade DT, Skilbeck CE, Langton-Hewer R. Selected cognitive losses after stroke. Frequency, recovery and prognostic importance. *Int Disabil Stud* 1989; **11**: 34–9.

40. Wade DT, Langton-Hewer R, Skilbeck CE, Bainton D *et al.* Controlled trial of home care service for acute stroke patients. *Lancet* 1985; **ii**: 323–6.

41. Wade DT, Langton-Hewer R. Outcome after an acute stroke: urinary incontinence and loss of consciousness compared in 532 patients. *Q J Med* 1985; **221**: 347–52.

42. Wade DT, Langton-Hewer R. Functional abilities after stroke: measurement, natural history and prognosis. *J Neurol Neurosurg Psychiatry* 1987; **50**: 177–82.

43. Wade DT, Parker V, Langton-Hewer R. Memory disturbance after stroke; frequency and associated losses. *Int Rehabil Med* 1986; **8**: 60–4.

44. Martin J, White A, Meltzer H. *Office of Population Censuses and Surveys. Disabled adults: services, transport and employment. Report 4, Disability in Greater Britain.* London: HMSO, 1989.

45. Wilkinson PR, Wolfe CDA, Warburton FG, Rudd AG *et al.* A long-term follow-up of stroke patients. *Stroke* 1997; **28**: 507–12.

46. Bunn F. The needs of families and carers of stroke patients. In: Wolfe C, Rudd A, Beech R (eds). *Stroke services and research.* Stroke Association, 1996.

47. Riddell JA. Out-of-hours visits in a group practice. *Br Med J* 1980; **i**: 1518–20.

48. Office of Population Censuses and Surveys. *Morbidity statistics from general practice, 1991–92.* London: HMSO, 1995.

49. Ebrahim S, Barer D, Nouri F. An audit of follow-up services for stroke patients after discharge from hospital. *Int Disabil Stud* 1987; **9**: 103–5.

50. Barer DH. Stroke in Nottingham: the burden of nursing care and possible implications for the future. *Clin Rehabil* 1991; **5**: 103–10.

51. Legh-Smith J, Wade DT, Langton-Hewer R. Services for stroke patients one year after stroke. *J Epidemiol Community Health* 1986; **40**: 161–5.

52. Oxfordshire Community Stroke Project. Incidence of stroke in Oxfordshire: first year's experience of a community stroke register. *Br Med J* 1983; **287**: 712–7.

53. Wolfe CD, Taub NA, Woodrow J, Richardson E *et al.* Patterns of acute stroke care in three districts of southern England. *J Epidemiol Community Health* 1993; **47**: 144–8.

54. Lindley RI, Amayo EO, Marsall J, Sandercock PAG *et al.* Hospital services for patients with acute stroke in the United Kingdom: the Stroke Association survey of consultant opinion. *Age Ageing* 1995; **24**: 525–32.

55. Gladman J, Albazzaz M, Barer D. A survey of survivors of acute stroke discharged from hospitals to private nursing homes in Nottingham. *Health Trends* 1991; **23**: 158–60.

4 Working group on stroke outcomes: report to the Department of Health

Anthony G Rudd

Chairman, Stroke Outcomes Working Group & Consultant Stroke Physician, Guys and St. Thomas's Hospital, London

The working group report to the Department of Health on stroke outcomes[1] aimed at identifying the key areas of stroke management and the measures that could be used to evaluate quality of care. As stroke is such a dominant cause of death and disability in the UK, there was considerable enthusiasm for developing indicators capable of producing an improvement in the standard of stroke care nationally.

Working group

The working group's membership included representatives from all the major professions involved in stroke care as well as representatives from patient and carer groups. It was important to involve as many different groups as possible in the development of potential indicators, some of which still lack a strong evidence base. As much of the decision-making was going to have to be based on professional consensus, the constitution of the group needed to be representative and include those with sufficient background knowledge to enable them to make recommendations that would be acceptable to their colleagues.

Choice of indicators

The outcome of a stroke is not like the outcome of a football match where the quality of the result is absolutely clear at the end. Successful stroke treatment may in some instances be effective palliative care, providing support to carers, while at the same time ensuring that the last days of the stroke victim's life are as comfortable as possible. High intensity medical treatment for a severely brain damaged person which results in survival, only in a vegetative state, may appear better in statistics of mortality but is probably not in the best interests of the patient. For one patient the main priority in recovery may be to regain mobility. For another it may not matter whether they can walk, but to be able to speak again may be of prime importance. Selection of outcome measures for a disease as variable in its pathology and severity as stroke, and affecting young and old with varying levels of pre-morbid function, was a challenging task. Evaluation of care also needs to be able to examine hospital and community care, short and long-term effects of the disease; both health and social services need to be involved. The effects of the stroke on the patient, carers and the community need all to be considered.

There are therefore problems identifying appropriate indicators for stroke. Many of the key areas of stroke care are unsupported by a strong evidence base on which to develop indicators and even where the evidence exists there are not always validated or feasible tools with which to measure outcome. For example there are a lot of unanswered questions and many uncertainties about the epidemiology of stroke. Measurement of an apparently simple indicator such as mortality, is fraught with difficulties. When is the best time after a stroke to measure death? At seven days the death is most likely to simply reflect the severity of the stroke, rather than anything about the quality of care. Thirty-day mortality is purely arbitrary and will be heavily influenced by the casemix of the unit being studied. If the policy of the unit is to discharge all patients to nursing homes at two weeks the 30-day mortality figures will appear excellent. If a stroke unit excludes all severe cases, again the mortality figures will be misleading. Clearly, data from community registers will be more reliable and informative, but such data are difficult and expensive to collect and for the majority of areas provide an impractical measure.

Stroke is not a single disease, its natural history is enormously variable, and not always explicable. Sometimes it is not clear why one patient will get better more quickly than any other. There is still difficulty in reaching a consensus about how to define casemix measures, which is a key area in interpreting any outcomes that are used. Patients are often elderly, and have significant co-morbidities which complicate the whole picture. Moreover, the influence of the environment is absolutely critical in determining appropriate treatment. If they live on their own in poor quality housing, clearly that is going to have a major impact upon their recovery and how they cope with impairment.

The working group has clearly documented their reasons for the choice of outcome indicators. For some there is concern about the sensitivity and the feasibility of the indicator. For example, considerable discussion centred around the use of the Barthel ADL score, a simple 20-point measure of disability. What does it really tell you about the patient? It is too crude to be of use to individual therapists monitoring the effect of treatment from week to week. Yet at least it is known that it can be collected reliably by a range of professionals, without an excessive amount of training and it is a measure widely understood within the stroke world. Thus the measure is feasible to collect, is likely to be reliable but may not be clinically useful.

The working group finally chose many process measures to be used as proxies for outcome. For example, the evidence from the stroke unit trials unequivocally shows that patients managed by a co-ordinated rehabilitation team either in a geographically-based stroke unit or as a team visiting the wards, do better. The indicator chosen was whether the patient was managed by a specialist multi-disciplinary team. Using the process measure as a proxy of outcome avoids the issue of casemix. It is more acceptable to clinicians than a true measure over which they may have much less control. Often the clinicians will take the opportunity to measure the process of care as a way of putting pressure on managers to provide more resources.

The working group divided its list of outcomes into those indicators that it considered could be measured on a routine basis in all Trusts and those that could be measured routinely in some areas, or intermittently in all or some areas. The decision as to which category an indicator fell into was related more to the feasibility of data collection within the health service at the moment than the importance the group attached to the measure. Patient satisfaction, carer burden, and patient knowledge of their disease, are areas where there needs to be considerably more work before they can be routinely measured. At present there are no adequate measures that could be routinely implemented and they are not stroke-specific.

Interpretation of results

Another crucial issue to be addressed is how the results are to be interpreted. Three examples are given to illustrate the difficulties that may be encountered. One study attempted to examine patient satisfaction within a stroke service. This study performed a satisfaction survey in two centres, one where there was a well co-ordinated stroke service where physicians, therapists and nursing staff felt that they were actually providing a good model of care, and one which was much less well co-ordinated in a smaller 'cottage hospital'. The patient satisfaction survey did not show any significant difference between the two services. Either the patients were not identifying what clinicians and the research literature identified as the good service or the tool was inadequate.

An important paper was published in 1996 by Davenport et al.[2] This paper looked at the influence of casemix measurement on outcome. Outcomes were measured in a hospital before and after the introduction of a stroke unit. Table 1 summarises the results from the study.

Table 1 Odds ratios (95% confidence intervals) comparing standard ward care with stroke service care; data for four outcomes before and after correction for age and sex only, and for 19 indicators of casemix. (Data from ref. 2). Reproduced by permission of the Br Med J.

Outcome			Standard care	Stroke unit care	Odds ratio	p value
Alive at 30 days	Uncorrected		162/215	214/250	0.5 (0.3 to 0.8)	0.007
	Age and sex				0.8 (0.6 to 1.0)	0.026
	Casemix				0.9 (0.6 to 1.2)	0.007
Alive at 12 months	Uncorrected		131/215	181/249	0.6 (0.4 to 0.9)	0.01
	Age and sex				0.8 (0.7 to 1.0)	0.046
	Casemix				1.0 (0.7 to 1.2)	0.744
Independent at 12 months	Uncorrected		51/213	89/245	0.6 (0.4 to 0.9)	0.006
	Age and sex				0.8 (0.6 to 0.9)	0.014
	Casemix				0.9 (0.7 to 1.3)	0.694
Living at home at 12 months	Uncorrected		91/215	152/249	0.5 (0.3 to 0.7)	<0.001
	Age and sex				0.7 (0.6 to 0.9)	0.001
	Casemix				0.9 (0.7 to 1.1)	0.252

0   0.2   0.4   0.6   0.8   1   1.2   1.4

The data was collected for those that were alive for 30 days and at 12 months, and those who were independent at 12 months and back home at 12 months. By looking at the data corrected for age and sex, the evidence shows that the introduction of the stroke unit produced a major benefit. Patients were surviving and doing so in a fitter state than before the stroke unit. However, when a more sophisticated model, including 19 measures of casemix were included, there turned out to be no difference before and after. The explanation for the apparently improved results must have been that over the period of study the admission policies to the hospital and stroke ward, or the type of strokes happening in the district changed.

The other example is from a BIOMED study[3] looking at practice in a range of hospitals around Europe including four centres in the UK, and hospitals in France, Germany, Spain, Hungary, Poland, Portugal, Latvia, Russia and Lithuania. This research study was able to collect casemix measures and death rates and Barthel scores at three months and one year after stroke. The study revealed that after adjustments for casemix there were very marked differences in outcome between centres. Unfortunately, the four UK centres had significantly lower Barthel scores and higher mortality rates at three months than many of the other centres in Europe. There are two possible interpretations: either casemix measurement was inadequate or else in the UK we are treating people significantly less effectively than they are elsewhere in Europe. The alternative explanation of poor quality or inaccurate data collection is too easy an explanation. The questions these data raise are whether similar data measured at a national level would be interpretable, and even if real differences could be identified, is there any point measuring them if we do not understand what it is about the care that results in such large differences in outcome?

Conclusion

A series of outcome measures have been produced to be considered for use by the Department of Health. They cover the spectrum of stroke care from primary prevention to the effect of disability on patient and carers quality of life. Many of the measures are process, which are not likely to be as acceptable to the Department of Health as true outcome measures. The underlying concern of clinicians with the whole process of outcome measurement is that league tables will be produced that do not accurately reflect quality of care. There is also concern about resources used in collecting these data. Nevertheless, it is important that clinicians participate in the process and agree measures that have a rational basis. If the clinicians do not drive the process the administrators are unlikely to do a better job.

References

1. Rudd A, Goldacre M, Amess M, Fletcher J *et al* (eds). *Health outcome indicators: Stroke. Report of a working group to the Department of Health.* Oxford: National Centre for Health Outcomes Development, 1999.

2. Davenport RJ, Dennis MS, Warlow CP. Effect of correcting outcome data for case mix: an example from stroke medicine. *Br Med J* 1996; **312**: 1503–5.

3. Wolfe CD, Tilling K, Beech R, Rudd AG *et al.* Variations in case fatality and dependency from stroke in western and central Europe. The European BIOMED Study of Stroke Care Group. *Stroke* 1999; **30**: 350–6.

5 The Royal College of Physicians Stroke Minimum Data Set

Penny Irwin

Research Associate, Clinical Effectiveness and Evaluation Unit, Royal College of Physicians, London

> Definition of a minimum data set:
>
> A widely agreed upon and generally accepted set of terms and definitions constituting a core of data acquired for medical records and employed for developing statistics suitable for diverse types of users and analyses
>
> Last JM. *A Dictionary of Epidemiology*, 1988

The Intercollegiate Working Group for Stroke comprises a multi-disciplinary team of professionals experienced in the area of stroke care. Its main purpose is to improve the consistency of standards of care following stroke by developing a practical data collection tool that would incorporate information about casemix. One of the first tasks therefore was to agree a minimum data set for stroke to be used as the basis for clinical audit, and to use casemix information to inform audit and outcomes data (Irwin & Rudd, 1998). The criteria for selection of the items was that they should be:

- specific to stroke
- predictive of outcome or help inform about outcome
- easy to collect and therefore few in number
- discreet indicators in their own right.

The selection process was followed by a period of intensive consultation and discussion which aimed to base the Minimum Data Set (MDS) on the best research evidence available. **Accurate outcome measurement requires an understanding of the extent to which recovery after stroke occurs naturally or as a result of treatment.**

> 'Variations in case mix have a crucial influence on the interpretation of outcome data, and this is particularly important in non-randomised comparative studies. Such studies, comparing performance within and between different provider units, are likely to become increasingly common in the newly reformed NHS. To allow for meaningful interpretation, these studies must try to correct for case mix' (Davenport *et al*, 1996).

The working group chose 14 main data items, beginning with the demographic items of age and gender, followed by the pre-stroke items measured in terms of the Barthel ADL scale, and then pre-stroke residential accommodation and whether or not the patient had a carer before their stroke. Also included were: clinical status in the acute phase; worst level of consciousness; side of body affected and urinary continence at one week. For the disease itself, the MDS was designed to obtain information about the existence of a previous stroke, or type of stroke in terms of clinical classification. (Table 1).

Table 1. Royal College of Physicians Stroke Minimum Data Set Evidence Base for Items

Items	Rationale	References
Demography		
Age	Age associated with severity of stroke is an important predictive factor for outcome, both in terms of mortality and resulting dependency.	Bamford *et al* (1990b); Westling *et al* (1990); Alexander (1994); Nakayama *et al* (1994)
Sex	Men are more likely to suffer a stroke, although gender does not seem to influence individual outcome.	Bamford *et al* (1988); Wade *et al* (1984)
Pre-stroke		
Living accommodation	Living accommodation pre stroke may influence discharge destination. Change in this at discharge may indicate increased dependency.	Glass *et al* (1993)
Carer	Whether or not someone has a carer to look after them following discharge may influence their place of discharge and ultimate level of handicap.	Glass *et al* (1993); Ween *et al* (1996b); Stroke Trialists Collaboration (1997a)
Functional level (Barthel)	Pre-existing functional disability may limit progress and affect the final outcome of rehabilitation.	Alexander (1994); Anderson (1994)
Acute clinical status following stroke		
Worst level of consciousness in first 24 hours	An indicator of initial disease severity affecting outcome.	Wade *et al* (1985); Goldstein & Matchar (1994)
Side of body affected	Indicates the area of brain affected, which may in turn influence the outcome of rehabilitation.	Wade *et al* (1984); Alexander (1994)
Urinary continence at one week	Persisting incontinence is associated with greater disease severity and worse outcome from rehabilitation.	Wade & Langton Hewer (1985); Barer (1989); Lincoln *et al* (1990); Ween *et al* (1996a)
Process measures		
Brain scan	Whether or not this was performed may be an indication of casemix, but also of the facilities available.	
Multi-disciplinary involvement	Organised multi-disciplinary care can influence outcome.	Stroke Unit Trialists Collaboration (1997a), (1997b)
Disease		
Type of stroke (Clinical classification)	The type of lesion will affect case fatality, speed of recovery and ultimate outcome.	Bamford *et al* (1990a); Ween *et al* (1996b)
Previous stroke	An indicator of greater disease severity. Residual functional deficits from a previous stroke will affect outcome of subsequent ones.	Anderson (1994)
Outcome measures		
Length of stay	Indicator of casemix in association with other factors. Also an indicator of the quality of care and/or local arrangements for discharge in the community.	Stroke Trialists Collaboration (1997a)
Mortality	Case fatality can be an indicator of casemix. It will increase with age, will be higher in haemorrhagic stroke, and where there is pre-existing dependency or disease.	Bamford *et al* (1990b); Stroke Trialists Collaboration (1997b)
Functional level (Barthel)	A measure of disability after stroke and the outcome of rehabilitation.	Anderson (1994); Stroke Trialists Collaboration (1997 a,b)
Destination on discharge	An indication of the level of dependency at discharge and/or local care provision.	Kelly-Hayes *et al* (1988); Stroke Trialists Collaboration (1997b)
Living with carer after discharge	Having a carer to live with after stroke may positively influence discharge destination and ultimate levels of handicap.	Kelly-Hayes *et al* (1988); Glass *et al* (1993); Stroke Trialists Collaboration (1997a)

This approach sought to work in harmony with what the service was already collecting, hence the decision to fit in with the ICD–10 disease classifications, and the European Stroke Database. There are two process measures within the MDS: (1) investigation by imaging, and (2) multi-disciplinary team involvement. Current evidence is pointing to the effectiveness of multi-disciplinary teams in stroke units, and the importance of involving these teams in the first week of care. This is a difficult area to measure and was delineated as: those members of the multi-disciplinary team who had contact with the patient within the first week of admission.

The nation-wide Sentinel Audit of Stroke undertaken by the Clinical Effectiveness and Evaluation Unit incorporated the MDS items into the audit proforma. A one-sided carbonated A4 MDS form was also developed so that one copy could be held in the casenotes for clinical information, and a second copy used by the clinical audit department for analysis (Fig 1). Put very simply, the Royal College of Physicians Minimum Data Set provides a way of gathering key data items to enable comparisons and evaluations.

Fig 1. RCP minimum data set for stroke.

ROYAL COLLEGE OF PHYSICIANS – STROKE MINIMUM DATA SET

DEMOGRAPHIC INFORMATION (FROM PAS)

NHS/(CHI Scotland) number: _____

Date of birth: _ _ _ _ _ _   Sex: M ❑   F ❑   Post code for usual address: _____

STROKE ONSET AND HOSPITAL STAY

1. Date of stroke: _ _ _ _ _ _	3. Date of discharge: _ _ _ _ _ _
2. Date of admission: _ _ _ _ _ _	4. Date of death: _ _ _ _ _ _

FUNCTIONAL STATUS — PRE-STROKE AND AT DISCHARGE   P = PRE-STROKE   D = AT DISCHARGE (please tick)

5. Living accommodation:	P	D		6. If living at home:	P	D
Independent housing	❑	❑		Lives alone	❑	❑
Warden controlled	❑	❑		Lives with spouse/carer	❑	❑
Residential/nursing home	❑	❑				
Hospital	❑	❑				

7. **Dependency:** (Barthel ADL Functional Assessment scale)

	P	D			P	D
Bowels	___	___		Mobility	___	___
Bladder	___	___		Transfer	___	___
Grooming	___	___		Dressing	___	___
Toilet use	___	___		Stairs	___	___
Feeding	___	___		Bathing	___	___

8. **Previous stroke:**   YES ❑   NO ❑

CLINICAL STATUS ON ADMISSION

9. Worst level of consciousness in 24 hours following stroke:		10. Side of body affected:	
Fully conscious	❑	No clear lateralising signs	❑
Drowsy (responds to speech)	❑	Right side	❑
Semi conscious (not fully rousable)	❑	Left side	❑
Unconscious (responds to pain only/no response)	❑	Both	❑

AT ONE WEEK

11. **Urinary continence at one week:**

0 = Incontinent/catheterised	❑
1 = Occasional accident (max. once per 24 hours)	❑
2 = Continent (over previous 48 hours)	❑

12. **Professionals who assessed the patient during the first week of admission?**

1 Doctor	❑	6 Speech and Language therapist	❑
2 Nurse	❑	7 Clinical Psychologist	❑
3 Physiotherapist	❑	8 Social Worker	❑
4 Occupational therapist	❑	9 Other	❑
5 Dietitian	❑		

13. **Brain Scan (CT/MRI) done?**   YES ❑   NO ❑   Requested not done ❑

14. **Clinical classification:**

1 Cerebral infarction	❑	4 Other	❑
2 Intracerebral haemorrhage	❑	5 Don't know	❑
3 Sub-arachnoid haemorrhage	❑		

References

Alexander MP. Stroke rehabilitation outcome: A potential use of predictive variables to establish levels of care. *Stroke* 1994; **25**: 128–134.

Anderson C. Baseline measures and outcome predictions. *Neuroepidemiology* 1994; **13**: 283–89.

Bamford J, Sandercock P, Dennis M, Warlow C *et al.* A prospective study of acute cerebrovascular disease in the community: the Oxfordshire Community Stroke Project. 1. Methodology, demography and incident cases of first-ever stroke. *J Neurol Neurosurg Psychiatry* 1988; **51**: 1373–80.

Bamford J, Sandercock, P, Dennis M, Burn J *et al.* A prospective study of acute cerebrovascular disease in the community: The Oxfordshire Community Stroke Project. 2. Incidence, case fatality rates and overall outcome at one year of cerebral infarction, primary intracerebral and subarachnoid haemorrhage. *J Neurol Neurosurg Psychiatry* 1990; **53**: 16–22.

Bamford J, Dennis M, Sandercock P, Burn J *et al.* The frequency, causes and timing of death within 30 days of a first ever stroke: the Oxfordshire Community Stroke Project. *J Neurol Neurosurg Psychiatry.* 1990; **53**: 824–29.

Barer DH. Continence after stroke: useful predictor or goal of therapy? *Age and Ageing* 1989; **18**: 183–91.

Davenport RJ, Dennis MS, Warlow CP. Effect of correcting outcome data for case mix : an example from stroke medicine. *Br Med J* 1996; **312**: 1503–5.

Glass TA, Matchar DB, Belyea M, Feussner JR. Impact of social support on outcome in stroke. *Stroke* 1993; **24**: 64–70.

Goldstein LB, Matchar DB. Clinical assessement in stroke. *J Am Med Assoc* 1994; **271**: 1114–20.

Iezzoni LI, Ash AS, Schwartz M, Daley J *et al.* Predicting who dies depends on how severity is measured: implications for evaluating patient outcomes. *Ann Intern Med* 1995; **123**: 763–770.

Irwin P, Rudd A. Casemix and process indicators of outcome in stroke: the Royal College of Physicians minimum data set for stroke. *J Roy Coll of Phys* 1998; **32**: 442–4.

Kelly-Hayes M, Wolf PA, Kanhel WB, Sytkowski P *et al.* Factors influencing survival and need for institutionalisation following stroke: The Framingham study. *Arch Phys Med Rehabil* 1988; **69**: 415–18.

Last JM. *A Dictionary of Epidemiology* (second edition); London: Oxford University Press, 1988.

Lincoln NB, Jackson JM, Edmans JA, Walker MF *et al.* The accuracy of prediction about progress of patients on a stroke unit. *J Neurol Neurosurg Psychiatry* 1990; **53**: 972–75.

Nakayama H, Jogensen HS, Raaschou HO, Olsen TS. The influence of age on stroke outcome: the Copenhagen Study. *Stroke* 1994; **25**: 808–813.

Stroke Unit Trialists' Collaboration. Collaborative systematic review of the randomised trials of organised inpatient (stroke unit) care after stroke. *Br Med J* 1997; **314**: 1151–1159.

Stroke Unit Trialists' Collaboration. How do stroke units improve patient outcomes? A collaborative systematic review of the randomised trials. *Stroke* 1997; **28**: 2139–2144.

Wade DT, Langton Hewer R, Wood VA. Stroke: influence of patient's sex and side of weakness on outcome. *Arch Phys Med Rehabil* 1984; **65**: 513–516.

Wade DT, Langton-Hewer R. Outcome after an acute stroke: urinary incontinence and loss of consciousness compared in 532 patients. *QJM* 1985; **221**: 347–52.

Ween JE, Alexander MP, D'Esposito M, Roberts M. Incontinence after stroke in a rehabilitation setting: outcome associations and predictive factors. *Neurology* 1996; **47**(3): 659–663.

Ween JE, Alexander MP, D'Esposito M, Roberts M. Incontinence after stroke in a rehabilitation setting: outcome associations and predictive factors. *Neurology* 1996; **47**(2): 388–392.

Westling B, Norving M, Thorngren M. Survival following stroke. A prospective population based study of 438 hospitalised cases with prediction according to subtype, severity and age. *Acta Neurol Scand* 1990; **81**: 457–463.

6 A public health perspective

Jonathan Mant

Senior Lecturer, Medical School, University of Birmingham

This presentation aims to do three things. First, to recap on some of the fundamentals of outcomes work and the context in which this work is being done. Second, to deal with some of the difficulties in interpreting the data. And third, to discuss how different people could interpret the results: assuming that the data are accurate and complete, what would we do with them then?

The importance of this work has been given considerable emphasis by the latest White Paper, *The New NHS*,[1] which switched the emphasis away from management systems that had been pre-occupied with measuring cost and efficiency, toward a renewed focus on being responsible and accountable for clinical outcome and quality. This is manifest in two main ways: (i) the emphasis on clinical governance which is a *New NHS* term; and (ii) a new National Performance Framework (Table 1). One of the key features of the new proposals is that Chief Executives of Trusts, whether they are medical or non-medical, will carry responsibility for clinical mistakes in their hospital. This will switch the onus of accountability firmly away from just finance and efficiency to incorporate quality of care issues. Trust Boards will expect to receive monthly reports on quality so there will be much more paper being pushed around.

Table 1. Context for considering stroke outcomes

i **Clinical governance**

'Require practitioners to accept responsibility for developing and maintaining standards within their local NHS organisations.'

'Chief Executives will carry responsibility for ensuring quality of services provided by NHS Trusts.'

'NHS Trust Boards will expect to receive monthly reports on quality.'

ii **New National Performance Framework**

'Due weight given to things that really matter .... cost and quality.'

The six areas of the National Performance Framework are:

- health improvement
- fair access
- effective delivery
- efficiency
- patient care experience
- health outcomes of NHS care

The indicators that have been piloted and are discussed in this publication focus largely on the effective delivery of appropriate health care and possibly health outcomes of the NHS, and deal also with efficiency. The NHS Executive provide some guidance in a discussion paper following the *New NHS* White Paper about the criteria for assessing these indicators.[1] First, the indicator needs to be substantially attributable to the NHS, so for example, a population death rate for stroke is an important indicator perhaps of the health of the population. Is it an important indicator of NHS performance? A population indicator for stroke fits into the wider perspective of what affects health other than just health care. In terms of performance indicators, the NHS Executive are particularly interested in indicators that are affected by health care. These need to be relevant and important to policy makers, health professionals, and managers. They should avoid perverse incentives, and be robust and reliable. There needs to be high coverage, and different results should reflect real differences in performance. The indicator needs to be sensitive to change. If there is a change in the quality of service and an indicator does not pick this up, then it is probably not a very good indicator. Finally, indicators need to be timely. To identify an indicator to fit all these criteria is a difficult task.

I will illustrate two of the problems: perverse incentives and robustness. Perhaps the most publicised data in the world on using outcomes to measure quality of care is related to cardiac surgery in the US where surgeon-specific mortality figures following coronary artery surgery have been published since 1989. Several papers have demonstrated that over time, using sophisticated risk adjustment systems, the risk adjusted mortality in the US for cardiac surgery has gone down in those centres monitored. Risk adjustment tries to get round the problem of variability in casemix. It might be anticipated that if you are monitoring outcome, surgeons might select people with less problems, and therefore better chances of survival. Table 2 would seem to suggest that exactly the opposite is taking place. In 1989, 0.4% of the patients who had coronary artery surgery apparently had renal failure, but this went up to 2.8% by 1991. Similar increases are observed in the prevalence of other risk factors in patients undergoing surgery. These figures show how suddenly, there became a value to recording the risk factors. Clearly, if the recording of your risk factors is increased, case adjusted mortality goes down. There is an issue here about data robustness and the importance of clear definitions of each of the risk factors (Table 2).

Table 2. Trends in the prevalence of reported risk factors in the cardiac surgery reporting system[2]

Risk Factor	Reported Prevalence		
	1989 %	1990 %	1991 %
Renal failure	0.4	0.5	2.8
Congestive heart failure	1.7	2.9	7.6
Chronic obstructive pulmonary disease	6.9	12.4	17.4
Unstable angina	14.9	21.1	21.8
Low ejection fraction (<40%)	18.9	23.1	22.2

While the data in Table 2 suggests that sicker patients were being operated on, in fact, what cardiologists and cardiac surgeons felt they were doing was the opposite. They felt they were operating on people who were less likely to be severely ill. In other words they felt they were selecting patients who were a better risk. This illustrates a perverse incentive. Use of mortality as an indicator had the unintended consequence of influencing selection of patients for surgery.

It is important when thinking about how to use outcome measures to consider what are the sources of variation. One is methodological: Are the data complete? Is the measure reliable? Is there consistency of the definition of the numerator?

For example, is a pressure sore in one part of the country the same as a pressure sore somewhere else? Consistency of the denominator is also very important. If the denominator in one part of the country is the number of patients on the stroke unit only whereas in another part of the country it represents all patients with stroke in the hospital, does that match with the numerator? There is also the influence of chance, casemix and quality of care to be considered. A simple way of thinking about whether an indicator is likely to be useful is if you intuitively feel that quality of care is likely to count for a substantial amount of variation. If so, it is probably worth deciding on that indicator. If however, the quality of care is not likely to account for much variation, it may be that after having adjusted for casemix and perfected the methodology, it may not be worth using that indicator. The work involved in adequately adjusting for casemix is very intensive and there is much academic debate about whether an adjustment is complete, whether the right things have been adjusted, and so on. Before going down the road of more complex casemix adjustment systems, therefore, it is necessary to ask if it is worth doing.

A key question to consider is whether the cost of collecting the data and ensuring its completeness, accuracy, and standardisation justifies the benefits that can be derived from using the data. In order to be clear about this, it is important to ascertain how the data are to be used. Everyone who collects the data should also attempt to use them; data collection alone is a very sterile procedure and will become a bureaucratic exercise with limited value, an extra bit of paper that is collected and filed along with the routine returns. We have an opportunity here to collect data that can really make a difference and to believe this will make it worth doing. If we can't persuade ourselves it is going to make a difference then it is probably not worth doing.

In order to think about how the data might be used, it is useful to think about who will be using it. There are many different groups with a potential interest in the data: patients, public, health care professionals, NHS Trust management, purchasers, primary care groups and health authorities, the NHS Executive, and also Ministers.

The pilot study data provide us with some idea of how the data might be used. Fig 1 shows a percentage of patients with a Barthel at discharge of <10 in five different units. It includes the five units that had the most recorded, along with confidence intervals. In unit A, 30% of patients were discharged for the Barthel of <10 ie severely disabled. In unit E, it was only 3% and the confidence intervals do not overlap. So even on this relatively small sample we seem to have significant differences between the characteristics of patients discharged from these units. What does it mean? The Barthel at discharge is not a clear directional indicator in that it is not immediately clear whether it is good to have a high rate, a high level of proportion of people discharged who are disabled, or a low rate.

Fig 1. Percentage of patients with Barthel at discharge <10

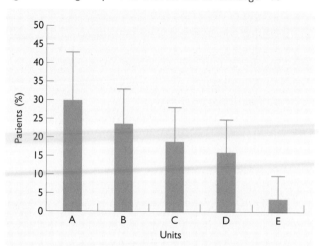

There are three major blocks of factors that could predict the Barthel at discharge as illustrated in Fig 2. There is the care in the hospital, including effectiveness of rehabilitation, length of stay, and survival rate. If severely disabled people within a unit die in hospital then the average discharge Barthel for that unit will tend to be higher. Discharge Barthel will also depend upon the availability of community services. The better the community services, presumably the more acceptable it will be to discharge patients who are moderately disabled. There are actually a number of potential uses of the Barthel measure (Table 3). For purchasers – if published alongside the length of stay and the discharge destination data the Barthel measure could inform discussion around provision of services of the primary/secondary care interface. If the relationship between purchaser and provider is going to move beyond financial discussions, this is possibly the type of information that might prove very useful. The Trust management might want to use it as an efficiency indicator: if there are people with high Barthel scores at discharge and a long length of stay, is that an indicator of the system going wrong somewhere? From the point of view of the health care professional, one of the rationales behind the Barthel measure is that they are prompted to think about different aspects of disability. If the disability exists on discharge, then hopefully they will plan on how those disabilities are going to be managed in the community.

Fig 2. What health care factors predict distribution of Barthel ADL at discharge from hospital?

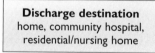

Discharge destination
home, community hospital,
residential/nursing home

Care in hospital
effectiveness of rehabilitation,
length of stay, survival rate

**Availability of community
services**
domiciliary or out-patient
therapy services, social services

Table 3. Potential use of Barthel Index at discharge

Purchasers: If published alongside length of stay and discharge destination data, may inform discussion around provision of services at primary/secondary care interface

Trust management: Efficiency of care – are there patients with high Barthel and long length of stay?

Health care professionals: Individual goal plans – are problems identified, acknowledged and addressed?

Patients and carers: Prognosis? Does Barthel at discharge (adjusted for time since stroke) have any predictive power?

Ministers and NHS Executive: Monitoring of policy at health/social care interface

Table 4. Incidence of pressure sores

- 13 pressure sores reported for 628 admissions (2%)
- Insensitive indicator
  - need 1626 patients per hospital to detect doubling of rate from 2% to 4%
  - need 614 patients per hospital to detect reduction in rate to 0%
  - need 208 patients per hospital to detect difference between 2% and 10%
- Therefore, not useful as a comparative indicator (given that would also need to adjust for casemix, length of stay etc).
  However, might be useful as a focus for 'critical incident' inquiry, if assumed that no patients with stroke should develop a pressure sore

Table 5. Swallowing assessment undertaken within 24 hours

- Range from 17% to 91%
- Potential uses:
  - Purchaser: can specify that this should take place (in 100%? OR which patients?)
  - Health care professionals: training issue
  - Trust management: clinical risk management issue
- Limited role for comparative data

If there were data to suggest how the patient might expect their Barthel to vary over time, it might be used prognostically. Hence, if it is known that this particular individual has a Barthel of 10, when he/she is discharged, can you give any information to them about how they might expect things to change over the next few months? That is obviously important information for the patient and for the carer.

For government and the NHS Executive, this sort of data could be used for monitoring the policy of the health care/social care interface. If social services are squeezed, does this mean that people are discharged from hospital with less disability? I can see that it would have a possible policy monitoring role as well.

Another indicator under discussion is the incidence of pressure sores (Table 4). The pilot study revealed that there were thirteen pressure sores reported out of 628 admissions (2%). It is not going to be a very sensitive indicator of differences in care. In order to detect a doubling of the pressure sore rate from 2% to 4% between hospitals, 1,626 patients per hospital would be needed in the study. For a reduction down to 0%, 614 patients would be needed. To detect differences of the magnitude that you are going to be detecting that are not due to chance, they are so big that you are going to think it is likely to be due to how pressure sores are defined and probably not to do with differences in quality. I suggest that the pressure sore rate is not useful as a comparative indicator, but could be useful as a focus for a critical incident enquiry. If you make the assertion that patients with stroke should not get pressure sores then every pressure sore can be viewed as a mistake. If there were an appropriate system in the hospital for learning lessons from these 'mistakes' in a non-confrontational positive way, that could be very useful.

The purchaser, might be interested in knowing that the Trust is measuring the pressure sore rate, but probably would not be particularly interested in the results. However, the Trust management ought to be very interested because it is relevant to clinical governance, although again, the rate should be of secondary importance. What is more relevant is what is done to find out why people are getting pressure sores in their hospital.

The item that is possibly the most sensitive, at least to the public, is the incidence of assessment of swallowing. If we say that everyone with stroke should be assessed for swallowing within 24 hours and we publish data indicating that some hospitals have only 17% of patients assessed, presumably a fairly simple thing to do, the national newspapers would have a field day: 'Hospitals can't even bother to measure swallowing in patients with stroke'. Care is therefore needed – though the national media can be a very powerful way of influencing change.

In conclusion, there is a strong impetus behind outcome work and it is no longer sufficient to focus only on the methodological limitations without trying to deal with the issue. We cannot stop the tide of outcome measurement in health care. It is important therefore to choose measures that we really think will be useful and to make sure they are used properly.

References

1. Department of Health. *The new NHS – modern, dependable: a national framework for assessing performance.* London, Stationery Office, 1997.

2. Green J, Wintfield N. Report cards on cardiac surgeons – assessing New York State's approach. *New Engl J Med* 1995; **332**: 1229–32.

7 Stroke outcome indicators – the pilot study

Andrew Georgiou

Research Associate, Clinical Effectiveness and Evaluation Unit

The aim of the stroke outcome pilot project undertaken by the Clinical Effectiveness and Evaluation Unit of the Royal College of Physicians was to test a selection of outcome indicators that relate to care and management of stroke patients in an acute setting.

The indicators chosen for the study specified a provider unit population made up of those admitted with a primary diagnosis of stroke, and measured:

- Distribution of the Barthel Index of Activities of Daily Living (ADL), at discharge from hospital

- Multi-professional involvement in the week following admission

- Percentage of patients for whom a formal swallowing assessment was undertaken within 24 hours of a stroke

- Incidence of pressure sores during the inpatient stay.

The piloting issues

The project identified a number of piloting issues that would form the basis of the investigation. These centred on questions such as the feasibility of collecting the data, the standardisation of the definitions used and an interpretation of the data gathered.

The study also aimed to assess the degree of reliability that could be attached to the results obtained as a means of judging their information value for the clinical management of patients. The work focused on the critical issue of the quality of the information. Is it robust? Is it complete? Is it meaningful? And what sort of policy should be adopted for data collection? This is linked to whether the data is worth collecting? And if so, whose job should it be, and what form should the collection take?

The study incorporated 14 sites which provided a geographical spread across England, particularly north and south of the country, and some variations in the size and type of unit involved, eg whether or not it was a stroke unit. The study also sought to compare sites according to their contrasting methods of data collection and organisational procedures.

How the data was collected?

At least 40% of the sites, used the Royal College of Physicians Minimum Data Set (see section 5), either directly for their data collection, or as a supplement to their own record keeping methods. Usually this meant adding their own fields to indicate whether or not a swallowing assessment had been undertaken, and using existing in-hospital procedures to measure pressure sore incidence. About 30% of sites actually established their own data collection forms, some of them through adapting the RCP Stroke Minimum Data Set. Over 20% of the sites used the European Stroke Database (ESDB) or an adapted version to collect the data.

A number of participating sites prepared papers and reports to document their results and provide their own evaluation of the indicators. They are particularly valuable in drawing attention to participants' own experiences and perceptions of the study and add a further dimension to an appraisal of the feasibility of data collection and the interpretation of results. Some of these contributions are presented below and the key points highlighted in Table 4. In some instances the pilot contributions have also included examples of the audit tools used to collect data.

The raw data

The findings were presented in the form of tables (see Tables 1 and 2) which helped to provide an initial overall picture. These figures represent the data available to the research team as of the project cut off point at the end of June 1998, and were used as the basis for a presentation of the results at the stroke outcomes seminar in July 1998. In some cases pilot sites extended their data collection studies beyond the cut off point.

Table 1. Stroke pilot study analysis

Hospital	Type of unit	*n*	Age (mean)	los (mean)
1	Stroke unit	18	69	47
2	Neurology ward	31	62	21
3	Stroke unit	32	76	26
4	Stroke unit	98	73	N/A
5	General	35	79	16
6	Stroke unit and General	144	74	26
7	General	68	77	51
8	Stroke team	32	N/A	25
9	Rehabilitation	15	72	20
10	General	92	72	38
11	Geriatric wards	70	80	21
12	General wards	40	78	39
13	Stroke unit	101	73	19
14	Elderly Care unit	50	86	37

Key: los = length of stay; N/A = not available

Notes

▌ The study included 14 sites and recorded 826 strokes. Generally the study sites provided data over a three-month period, although some sites contributed data for shorter periods.

▌ The mean age of stroke patients over the whole study came close to 75 years and varied from a mean of 62 within a neurology ward, to a mean of 86 at an elderly care unit.

▌ The mean length of stay was close to 30 days but ranged from 14 days at the elderly care unit, to over 50 at a hospital which runs a stroke service with a stroke team that assesses each patient admitted to the hospital with acute stroke.

Table 2. Results of pilot study

Hospital	Swallowing assessed within 24 hours		Incident pressure sores during admission		Multi-professional involvement in 1st week						Barthel ADL Index at discharge <10	
					OT	Phys	SW	SaLT	D	N		
	No.	%	No.	%	%	%	%	%	%		No.	%
1	4/17	24	0/2	0	89	72	6	39	22	18	3/14	21
2	8/30	27	0/30	0	3	87	0	29	13	31	4/27	15
3	4/15	27	0/26	0	53	87	9	50	28	32	1/30	3
4	51/98	52	3/98	3	70	81	N/A	55	N/A	73	17/57	30
5	21/23	91	N/A	–	57	94	0	74	5	35	N/A	–
6	25/144	17	2/144	1	11	54	1	28	13	144	20/82	24
7	N/A	–	2/68	3	93	100	72	71	65	68	12/45	27
8	20/32	62	2/32	6	94	100	19	72	12	32	3/23	13
9	N/A	–	0/15	0	13	100	0	40	0	15	0/12	0
10	N/A	–	N/A	–	17	69	0	21	21	92	12/73	16
11	18/39	46	3/43	7	13	55	0	56	3	67	6/12	50
12	22/36	61	0/31	0	37	67	2	7	2	35	7/23	30
13	45/72	63	0/89	0	12	92	9	70	23	78	13/71	18
14	9/50	18	1/50	2	20	48	N/A	36	22	50	N/A	–

Key

OT = occupational therapist; Phys = physiotherapist; SW = social worker; SaLT = Speech & Language Therapist; D = dietitian; N = patient denominator for multi-professional involvement; N/A = not available. Only in 2 of the hospitals had any patients seen by a clinical psychologist, so this profession is excluded from the table

Notes

▌ Since data were not complete for every hospital, the number of patients included varies for the different indicators.

▌ The highest percentage of swallowing assessment within 24 hours was recorded as 91% in a unit which recorded 23 cases. The lowest percentage was 18% in a hospital with 50 cases.

▌ Half of the units did not record any incidence of pressure sores during admission, however two units recorded pressure sore incidence at above 5%.

▌ Apart from doctors and nurses, the pilot sites generally documented physiotherapists as the discipline most often involved in the care of stroke patients. The least recorded were social workers and clinical psychologists. The highest percentage of Barthel score less than 10 (indicating severe and very severe dependence) was 45%. In most sites, between one-fifth to one-third of stroke patients were scored in this category.

Data collection

A data collection rate was established based on the percentage of data collected for each of the candidate indicators. Hence, if data was completed for all patients, a rate of 100% was achieved. If it were completed for only half the patients, the rate would be 50% and so on.

This measurement provided some idea of the potential difficulties involved in collecting the data but also posed some questions for further discussion and investigation.

Table 3. Stroke pilot data collection analysis

	Barthel %	Pressure sores %	Swallow test (24 hours)	Multi-professional involvement %
Minimum	14	4	17	78
Maximum	100	100	100	100
Mean	77	71	78	96

Notes

▌ Multi-professional involvement had the highest collection rate. Most of the pilot sites were able to achieve a 100% rate in collecting these data.

▌ The least successful collection rate was for pressure sores.

▌ The completeness rate for swallowing assessment data varied widely between hospitals.

Reasons for variation (See also Table 4).

There were a number of reasons that may explain the variation in the figures. The main ones, as identified by pilot sites, can be listed in the following categories:

Standards and procedures: The existence of standardised and well-defined procedures within the unit generally improved the quality of the data.

Existing data base: Sites with a pre-existing well-established data base eg European Stroke Data Base generally had higher collection rates.

Hospital wide documentation: Many sites have hospital-wide systems for recording prevalence and incidence of pressure sores. But there are varying opinions among sites about the quality of their respective systems.

Team approach: In some cases, units emphasised the importance of a centralised and widely understood approach particularly when it came to collecting information for swallowing assessments and pressure sores. Data collection was generally thought to be better if there was a pre-existing hospital-wide guideline in place, or awareness about such issues as dysphasia or pressure sores.

Conversely, *low collection* rates were often affected by:

Lack of co-ordination: This problem was highlighted by a Stroke Rehabilitation Unit who reported that no one person was responsible for co-ordinating the data collection.

Resources: One site reported that the size of the job had a major effect on data quality – the task of supplying information is very involved and can become cumbersome and almost impossible to maintain without the proper resources.

Time: One hospital noted that Barthel proved to the most time consuming measure. It could take between 10 and 15 minutes per patient particularly if you have to rely on retrospective collection.

Proper systems: The Specialist Registrar at one of the sites stated that different note keeping systems often complicated the data collection process and could make information impossible to decipher, comprehend or sometimes even find.

Clear aims and objectives: One hospital described the importance of clearly stated aims and objectives as a key factor affecting the quality of data.

An analysis of the key themes and issues arising from the pilot study can be summarised as follows:

The need for standardised and comparable data

The data collection process needs to be precisely defined to eliminate alternative interpretations and thereby ensure standardised and comparable data. The pilot study indicator that caused most discussion and variation was swallowing assessment. Many sites were unclear about what actually constitutes a swallowing assessment. Alternatively those sites that reported the existence of a well-defined hospital-wide schemes generally recorded a higher percentage of returns for this indicator. One site noted that clear operational definitions is one way to reduce the risks of inter-rater variation. Another site examined the results of their pilot study against their hospital's Hospital Episode Statistics (HES) ICD-10 data and found that many patients were missing from their study. This indicated the type of problems likely to be encountered when hospital-wide analyses are attempted.

The need for data collection to be simple, meaningful and accessible

The Stroke Minimum Data Set (or alternatively the European Stroke Data Base) were regarded as positive aids for data collection, enabling straightforward data entry and analysis. The value of a minimum data set is that it is a widely agreed upon, and generally accepted set of terms and definitions constituting a core of data for diverse types of users and analyses. The items that make up a minimum data set should therefore relate to key guidelines and recommendations, and include the 'need to know' items, as opposed to the 'nice to know' items.

It was generally recognised that data were of better quality when collected as close to the patient and time of treatment as possible. Many sites noted the importance of the person responsible for collecting the data. One unit reported that the most accurate Barthel reading was obtained when collected by the Stroke Co-ordinator, this is because they are able to follow up the patient as a matter of course. One hospital used physiotherapists for collecting data because they assess every stroke patient admitted and were familiar and experienced in the need for accurate and timely information.

The quality of data collection improves when it is shown to be meaningful, ie understandable, seen to be useful and defined in terms of purpose. Another dimension to this issue is the accessibility of data. Clinical ownership of data improves when it is available to those who require it, at the time that it is required.

Details of the experiences and results of the pilot sites are given on pages 41–73. Table 4 provides a digest of the main points.

Table 4 Key points from pilot studies

1. **Barthel scores**

   ▌ Not used universally and is difficult to collect where not used routinely as a clinical tool

   ▌ When needed to be collected as an outcome measure it is feasible to introduce it as a part of routine clinical practice

   ▌ Without a stroke severity measure to accompany the Barthel Index, interpretation is difficult

2. **Swallowing**

   ▌ Definition of what constitutes a formal swallowing assessment is needed. Such an assessment should not need to be conducted by a Speech and Language Therapist

   ▌ The importance of the introduction of a swallow screening procedure for use by doctors and nurses

3. **Multi-professional involvement**

   ▌ Easier to determine this outcome measure where units have joint notes or easy access to each profession's notes

   ▌ The data is difficult to collect where patients move between departments

   ▌ There is doubtful relevance of including social work referral in the first week

4. **Pressure sores**

   ▌ Difficulty in determining the best way of establishing accurate data without individual patient examination

   ▌ Heavily dependent on patient casemix

   ▌ Difficulty in determining whether pressure sores are community or hospital acquired

Overall

There were a number of cases where the practice in individual Trusts has been influenced by the need to collect outcome data. This may indicate that quality of care can itself be improved by the need to measure outcome.

CHAPTER 7 (continued)

Papers and studies of contributing pilot sites

Aim: Using the Royal College of Physicians minimum data set, to pilot a selection of indicators in the area of stroke that relate to the care and management of stroke patients in acute settings.

Source: Leicester Royal Infirmary NHS Trust: Stroke Services

Authors: Diane Cherry, (Stroke Research Nurse); Frazer Underwood, (Keyworker – Acute Stroke Unit); Mark Ardron, (Consultant Physician)

Acknowledgements: Val Collyer, Speech and Language Therapist, Fosse Healthcare NHS Trust

Background

The Leicester Royal Infirmary NHS Trust (LRI) has approximately 600 strokes admitted each year. We have a six-bed acute stroke unit (ASU) and a 24-bed specialist rehabilitation ward. The Royal College of Physicians Minimum Data set form was piloted on 149 patients admitted either to the ASU ($n=57$) or general medical wards ($n=91$) during three months from December 1997 to February 1998. One patient died in Accident & Emergency. Data was collected by the stroke research nurse and was taken mostly from medical and nursing records.

Early death and dependency

Since we studied *all* patients admitted to our hospital we have obviously included some patients who had suffered very severe strokes. These patients died shortly after admission and the amount of data on these individuals was limited as a result. Patients admitted to the general medical wards were more likely to have extensive strokes and consequently a poorer outcome and higher mortality rate.

Completeness of data

The main observation was that the amount of data the research nurse was able to collect and the time and effort involved was directly related to where the patient had been admitted.

Information was more concise and readily available for those patients admitted to our ASU where a multi-disciplinary stroke care pathway (CPW)[1] and documentation had been developed, as opposed to general medical wards who were not geared up to document the type of information required. The form was easy to use on the stroke unit and rehabilitation ward, and data was usually complete for patients cared for in these areas.

Data collection may have been better if we had chosen to let ward staff fill in the forms but this is undoubtedly reliant on their compliance, which may be poor when working under the stressful conditions of a busy medical ward, or if they see no obvious advantage.

Clinical classification

In the absence of a CT/MRI scan, clinical classification was on occasions difficult to record. If there was any doubt, a classification of 'other' was applied, although this may give the impression that a stroke was not the confirmed diagnosis when it clearly was. Therefore, a classification of '*Stroke ? type*' may be better, as used on the European Stroke Data Base.

Outcome measures

Barthel ADL

The Barthel ADL assessment is not used on our general medical wards. Attempts to elicit information on level of functioning from other sources were made, but this was time consuming and little was gained. Therefore data was often incomplete for patients on these areas.

Swallowing assessment within 24 hours

The ASU has developed its own screening tool known as ISSAC (Initial Safe Swallowing Ability Check) (see Table 1), which is applied to every patient admitted to the ASU by trained nursing staff. On the ISSAC form, only the date of the screen is documented and not the time. Therefore, it is possible that some are carried out after 24 hours although there is likely to be few in this area. Following this initial screen, appropriate referrals are made to the Speech and Language Therapist (SALT) for continuing dysphagia management.

The main discussion arises when one considers what constitutes a formal swallowing assessment. Is our ISSAC, as its title suggests: 1) simply a check to reduce the risk of aspiration pneumonia in those patients with an unsafe swallow, which should be followed by a formal swallowing assessment by a SALT? or, 2) is it, as some would suggest, acceptable as a formal swallowing assessment carried out by a registered nurse?

If we take the former view, that a formal swallowing assessment is one undertaken by a SALT, then no one is likely to have one within 24 hours. Alternatively, if the latter view is true, then we can say that all patients admitted to the ASU are likely to have a swallowing assessment within 24 hours, including unconscious patients who would fail the assessment at the first stage when the question is asked: *'Is the patient alert/responsive?'* and hence placed nil by mouth. This highlights another issue as many believe that a swallowing assessment can be undertaken only on patients who are conscious and able to co-operate.

We believe that whilst ISSAC may only be a screening tool it nevertheless ensures that all patients are protected from aspiration pneumonia which is surely the major aim of any such assessment.

Patients on general medical wards rarely have swallowing ability checked or formally assessed within 24 hours of admission as they are reliant on staff making urgent referrals to either ASU staff or SALT. Of the 91 patients admitted to the general medical wards during the study, no one had either a formal swallowing assessment or ISSAC documented as having been performed within 24 hours. However, some patients were deemed safe to take oral fluids and diet on the strength that they have an intact gag reflex, although this has been proven to be an unreliable method of ascertaining a patient's ability to swallow safely.[2]

Multi-professional involvement

Multi-professional involvement during the first week after a stroke was easy to measure on the ASU where the multi-disciplinary CPW was used. However, general medical wards were more difficult as therapists kept separate records, documenting only specific issues in the medical or nursing notes. Referrals were not well documented and often unreliable. The only way of gaining accurate information would have been to get authority to examine the therapists written records which would ultimately lead to unacceptable increases in time and work load.

Pressure sores

The incidence of pressure sores is believed to be poorly reported by staff. The hospital database used to audit the incidence of pressure sores was examined to pick up any of our study patients. If there was evidence of pressure sore development in the nursing or medical records this was also documented. Despite our finding no discrepancies between the two sources it is unlikely that this data was completely accurate.

Discharge

Poor notification of discharge, despite methods employed to prevent this, was a problem especially on general medical wards. Consequently, medical records were not readily available for review and staff were unable to provide reliable information on discharge status. Notes had to be traced which was particularly time consuming and often difficult if patients had been discharged to community hospitals. Even when notes had been retrieved, the information gained was of little value.

Conclusion

The Leicester Royal Infirmary's experience on collecting the proposed minimum data on stroke is that success depends on limiting data collection to specialist stroke areas. In these areas it is feasible for an individual to collect all the necessary information without expending unreasonable amounts of time and effort doing so.

The amount and quality of data collected was enhanced by employing a research nurse to carry out data collection, although whether it is cost effective to do so, especially when covering general medical wards, is another issue, as is job satisfaction. Maybe it is more appropriate to make this sort of data collection a multi-disciplinary team effort where collection is aided by incorporating all the necessary information into a care pathway.

References

1. Underwood F, Parker J. Developing and evaluating an acute stroke care pathway through action research. *Nurse Researcher* 1999; 1(2): 27–38.

2. Scottish Intercollegiate Guidelines Network. *A National Clinical Guideline recommended for use in Scotland by the Scottish Intercollegiate Guideline Network (SIGN)*. III: Identification and management of dysphagia. Edinburgh: SIGN, 1997.

Table 1. Initial safe swallowing ability check

▌ Follow each stage of this screening assessment
▌ If X is scored at any stage STOP assessment and re-assess in 24 hours and keep patient Nil by Mouth
▌ If there are still swallowing difficulties refer to Speech and Language Therapist (SALT)
▌ To respond to questions, mark = or X in the boxes please

	On admission	Day One		On admission	Day One
1. Is the patient alert/responsive?	☐	☐	3. Can the patient cough?	☐	☐
2. Is the patient able to sit upright?	☐	☐	4. Does the voice sound clear? (not wet or gurgly)	☐	☐

	Is there upward laryngeal movement? On admission	Day One	Does the patient swallow without coughing (wait 1 min after swallow) On admission	Day One	Is the voice clear 'say aah' On admission	Day One
5. Give a teaspoon of water	☐	☐	☐	☐	☐	☐
6. Repeat teaspoon of water	☐	☐	☐	☐	☐	☐
7. Repeat teaspoon of water	☐	☐	☐	☐	☐	☐
8. Give sip of water from glass	☐	☐	☐	☐	☐	☐
9. Repeat sip of water from glass	☐	☐	☐	☐	☐	☐
10. Repeat sip of water from glass	☐	☐	☐	☐	☐	☐

If patient completes assessment successfully, commence oral fluids

Recommended Diet

Normal fluids	☐	Soft diet	☐
Thickened fluids	☐	Pureed diet	☐

O/A ☐ Signed _____ Designation _____ Date _____

Day one ☐ Signed _____ Designation _____ Date _____

O/A = on admission

NEUROLOGY PROCESS, LEICESTER ROYAL INFIRMARY NHS TRUST 1998

Acknowledgement: Speech and Language Therapy Department, Fosse Healthcare NHS Trust

Aim: To pilot a selection of indicators in the area of stroke that relate to the care and management of stroke patients in an acute setting.

Source: Stoke Mandeville Hospital NHS Trust

Authors: Chris Durkin (Consultant Physician), Fiona Brockwell (Stroke Co-ordinator)

The information about stroke patients was collected from 1 January 98 until 31 March 98
Number of patients = 68; male 22 (32%); female 46 (68%); age range 45–97;
mean age 77 years.

Multi-disciplinary team working

The Stroke Mandeville Stroke Team is a mobile stroke team currently providing rehabilitation for all patients admitted with an acute stroke. Patients are in any of our six medical wards, two elderly rehabilitation wards and any outlying wards (Orthopaedics, Surgery, Gynaecology and Ophthalmology). Although the numbers of patients receiving care vary, we usually have between 25 to 30 patients on a regular basis. The team meets weekly and all referrals are directed through the Stroke Co-ordinator.

Multi-disciplinary team referral

Initially the stroke co-ordinator takes the referral then notifies the other members of the team, depending on presentation of symptoms. Our standard states that the patient assessment must begin within 24 hours of admission (or the next working day). The co-ordinator checks the daily bed state for new admissions, and can be reached on a bleep or answer machine service for direct referral.

If dysphagia is suspected, the patient remains nil by mouth until a swallowing assessment is performed. This assessment is completed by a dysphagia trained nurse, stroke co-ordinator or a speech and language therapist and usually takes place within 24–48 hours of admission; however, this greatly depends on the patient's conscious level.

Fig. 1 Presentation of symptoms

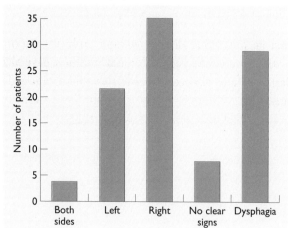

Barthel scores

Pre-morbid scores

The majority of patients, 54 (79%), had a score between 16–20.
9 (13.2%) had a score between 10–15; 3 (4.4%) had scores between 6–10; 2 (2.9%) had scores between 0–5.

Scores at 1 week

The majority of patients, 26 (38%), had scores between 0–5.
9 (13%) had scores between 6–9; 8 (12%) had scores between 16–20; 19 (28%) had scores between 10–15; 6 (0.9%) patients had died at this stage.

Discharge Barthel excluding 7 inpatients

The majority of patients, 17 (38%), had a Barthel score between 16–20.
15 (34%) patients had a score between 10–15; 9 (20%) had a score between 0–5; 3 (6.8%) had a score between 6–9.

Continence

Pre-stroke: 56 patients (82%) were continent, only 3 (4%) patients presented with catheters on admission to Stoke Mandeville Hospital.

12 (17.5%) of our patient group were experiencing continence problems before admission with their stroke.

Two patients who died within the first week were catheterised.

At one week: 21 (33%) of our patients were catheterised, 15 (23%) were regularly incontinent. 6 (9.5%) were occasionally incontinent. Only 24 (38%) of our patients were continent at this time.

We do not have a continence service at Stoke Mandeville Hospital. It could be suggested that our high incidence of catheterisation could be attributed to manual handling regulations, pressure sore prevention, low staffing levels and lack of product choice.

A catheter is often viewed as preserving dignity without truly considering the long-term complications which can arise. Our stroke patients do not routinely have bladder scanning or intermittent catheterisation. We have devised a simple assessment tool which may influence choice for continence management. There is also an incontinence resource file (introduced in May 1998) on every acute area which may assist in decision making.

Fig 2. Continence levels

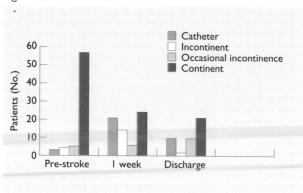

Pressure sores

Only 2 of the 68 patients had pressure sores. One patient had been lying on the floor for at least 24 hours prior to admission to hospital. Their pressure sore was rated grade 3 on the Stirling Scale (ie full thickness skin loss involving damage or necrosis of subcutaneous tissue, but not extending to underlying bone, tendon or joint capsule). This patient scored 25 on the Waterlow risk assessment and a Nimbus alternating mattress was used as per Aylesbury Vale Pressure Care Policy and Guidelines, 1996. The sore improved, but the patient died.

The second patient had broken her ankle at the stroke onset and was found to have a grade 3 Stirling Scale sore upon removal of a Plaster of Paris. She scored 24 on the Waterlow scale and was also nursed on a Nimbus Mattress.

30 patients were assessed using the Waterlow Risk Tool. The scores ranged from 24 to 11.

We believe our low incidence of sores is directly influenced by our 10-point pressure care policy, our Tissue Viability Nurse and the equipment library allowing prompt access to specialised equipment.

Problems encountered

▌ Our patients are admitted to an admissions ward, transferred to a consultant-based ward then transferred to an elderly rehabilitation ward, or off-site specialist rehabilitation unit for the under-65s (depending on rehabilitation potential). It is difficult to keep up to date on a daily basis.

▌ We have an extensive hospital site and our patients can be on 12 different wards.

▌ Wastage of time travelling to and from different wards for all members of the team.

▌ No clerical support to produce collection forms and distribute them.

▌ Stroke link nurses were able to assist in collecting information, however it was difficult to arrange time to discuss the project with them individually. Some were more keen to become involved in the project than others.

▌ No assistance to put information onto the data base.

▌ Duplication of information (this was partly our own fault as we had not clarified how the information would be passed on).

▌ The pilot was helpful as it identified deficits in continence management which we are currently working on.

Table 1. Guidelines/procedures for dysphagia management
Stoke Mandeville Hospital NHS Trust: Speech and Language Therapy Department

Purpose of Guidelines:

All dysphagia patients are given the opportunity to receive adequate nutrition in a safe manner acceptable to them.

Standards / Outcomes

▌ The patient receives an assessment within 2 days of the problem being identified

▌ The patient's nutritional support is maintained at an agreed level

▌ The patient does not contract an aspiration-related chest infection

▌ The patient/patient's family receive an information leaflet

Guidelines:

▌ If a patient is admitted with a stroke, and is identified by doctors/nurses as having potential swallowing problems, the patient should be seen by a *Dysphagia Trained Nurse*

▌ The *Dysphagia Trained Nurse* will carry out a screening assessment, completing:
  – *Ward Screening Assessment Summary Form* (placed in nursing notes)
  – *Dysphagia Assessment Summary* (placed in the patient's medical notes with a copy to Speech and Language Therapy)
  – *Feeding Management Plan* (posted above patient's bed with a copy to Speech and Language Therapy)

▌ The Dysphagia Trained Nurse will also give the patient the leaflet *Dysphagia: Information for Patients and Relatives.*

▌ The result of the *Dysphagia Trained Nurse's* assessment will be one of the following:
  – ward management of the patient's feeding
  – referral to Speech and Language Therapy for complex feeding problems
  – referral to Dietetics

▌ If there are no *Dysphagia Trained Nurses* available to carry out a screening assessment, the patient should be referred to Speech and Language Therapy.

▌ All patients with swallowing problems as a consequence of progressive neurological conditions (ie not stroke) should be referred immediately to Speech and Language Therapy for assessment and management.

Aim: Pilot of a selection of stroke outcome indicators

Source: Heatherwood and Wexham Park Hospitals Trust

Authors: Shelagh Gowing, (Neurology Specialist Nurse) and Mary Price, (Occupational Therapist)

Factors impacting pilot project results

- Outcome indicators chosen felt to be nursing specific, which resulted in the nurse co-ordinator taking full responsibility for data collection.

- Due to anticipated workload on nurse co-ordinator, data collection was concentrated on one site only.

- Only patients who were referred to the 'Stroke Rehab Team' were included in pilot project – ie only those patients who would benefit from intensive rehabilitation.

- The Trust has a very active fast access neurovascular clinic which has a large impact on the number of patients requiring admission to hospital.

Outcome indicator 1:
Patients within a provider unit for whom a swallowing assessment was undertaken within 24 hours of a stroke

Findings

Of the 32 patients looked at in the three-month project, 20 patients received a formal swallow assessment within 24 hours of admission to Wexham Park Hospital.

Definition of formal assessment: It was decided that a formal assessment was one undertaken by the Speech & Language Therapist or a Dysphagia Trained Nurse.

Assessments undertaken by a medic and indicated in the notes as assessed and safe to take oral hydration and nutrition were also included, though those recorded as having a 'gag reflex' were not recorded as having been formally assessed.

Influencing factors: December 1997 saw our first Dysphagia Training Course for qualified nurses, we have thus far trained and assessed 20 nurses working within the Stroke Units and the Medical Assessment Units.

Interpretation: Dysphagia is looked at using a team approach within our Trust, the pilot project results have prompted us to look at dysphagia training across the entire Medical Unit.

Outcome indicator 2:
Incidence of pressure sores during the inpatient stay within a hospital provider population with a primary diagnosis of stroke

Findings

Of the 32 patients looked at in the three-month project, two patients developed pressure sores during their stay at Wexham Park Hospital.

Grading scale used: Waterlow Pressure Sore Prevention / Treatment Scoring Scale.

Influencing factors: The low number of sores recorded in this data sample is probably influenced by the fact that those patients who are suitable for intensive rehabilitation are not those with high risk Waterlow Scores.

Interpretation: Our Trust now has a Tissue Viability Group looking at issues of pressure sore care Trust-wide, we have recently completed a pressure sore prevalence study and a Trust-wide mattress renewal program.

Outcome indicator 3:
Multi-professional involvement in the week following admission with a primary diagnosis of stroke within a provider unit population

Findings

Doctor	100%	Dietitian	12.5%
Nurse	100%	SALT	71.8%
Physiotherapist	100%	Clinical psychologist	0%
Occupational therapist	94%	Social worker	18.7%

Indicators of assessment: written confirmation in medical notes or nursing notes.

Influencing factors: patients referred to the 'Stroke Team' within our Trust indicates automatic referral to the multi-disciplinary team.

Interpretation: to avoid time delay before assessment by multi-professionals we now have weekly multi-disciplinary meetings which are attended by the disciplines indicated above. These meetings provide access to fast assessment by the Dietitian, Clinical Psychologist and Social Worker

Outcome indicator 4:
Distribution of the Barthel Index of Activities of Daily Living (ADL), at discharge from hospital, within a provider unit population with a primary diagnosis of stroke

Findings

Level of dependence on discharge	Percentage of 23 discharge patients (6 were inpatients at time of final report, 3 patients died)
Very severe dependence	8.7
Severe dependence	4.3
Moderate dependence	21.7
Mild dependence	52.2
Independent	13.0

Indicators of assessment: Barthel calculated on nursing notes and care plan information.

Influencing factors: patients referred to the 'Stroke Team' are those felt suitable for intensive rehabilitation.

Interpretation: this project has led to the establishment of a weekly multi-disciplinary meeting for the collection and standardisation of Barthel scores.

Aim: Testing stroke outcome indicators in the real world

Source: Leeds Teaching Hospital NHS Trust (St James's University Hospital)

Authors: E Jackson, JM Bamford

Leeds Stroke Database (Authors: P Brunyee, JM Bamford, J Fear)

- The Leeds Stroke Database was established in 1994 to compile an ongoing register of all patients who have suffered a stroke in the Leeds area and to collect outcome data as part of the routine NHS service. The outcome measure is based on the Barthel Index.

- Data collection commenced from the Leeds hospitals in 1994, from district nurses in 1996, and from GPs since 1997.

- The benefits of having the stroke database are:
  1. The provision of anonymised, accurate and comprehensive data to the Health Authority for stroke service planning.
  2. The communication of the outcome data to both the patient's GP and hospital consultant.
  3. It is available as a case register to facilitate stroke research in Leeds.

- Additionally, the database personnel are involved in planning a rolling programme of stroke study afternoons for health and social services staff in Leeds.

Practical application of stroke outcome indicators

The indicators were applicable to all stroke patients admitted within the hospital, although not all patients with a diagnosis of stroke are admitted to one particular ward. It was the different documentation procedures within the hospital's directorates that determined the quality and collection of the required information. It soon became apparent that obtaining data would be difficult because of these variations in practice. The pilot work was therefore conducted within the neurology department, where the use of an adaptation of the RCP minimum data set proforma assisted the collection of information. Data was collected by the research nurse to ensure consistency.

Formal swallowing assessment within 24 hours of hospital admission

- Is a physical demonstration required from all patients or can they be assessed using questioning alone? Clarification of question is necessary and by whom should the assessment be undertaken?

- Primarily performed by the medical staff and documented within the medical notes. Occasionally performed by the nursing staff.

- Not routinely seen by the speech therapist.

Multi-professional involvement in the first week following hospital admission

- Ambiguity occurs if a patient is transferred from another department; is the first week of admission from hospitalisation or from arrival to the neurological unit?

- This indicator demonstrated areas for future investigation, highlighted the inefficiency of the referral system and identified which therapists were routinely involved acutely and which were not.

- Different therapists document in different sets of notes which were not always accessible to the medical/nursing notes staff.

Distribution of the Barthel Index of Activities of Daily Living at discharge

- Difficult to obtain due to differing documentation procedures.

- Only the neurological ward used the Barthel Score within the medical directorate.

- Severity of stroke is not documented, therefore no measurement of progress is established.

- Barthel score documented by the medical staff. However, it is the nursing staff and therapists who assist with the ADLs. Would they be more appropriately placed to perform the score?

Hospital acquired pressure sores

- All patients are assessed using the Waterlow score on admission, carried out by the nursing staff. Patients at risk are identified early and pressure relieving devices initiated.

- Despite using this tool not all sores present on admission were documented, making it difficult to determine that they were not hospital acquired.

To conclude

Routine documentation procedures used by the doctors, nurses and other therapists within neurology, significantly assisted the collection of data for the above indicators. The use of these standardised forms enabled greater consistency of data and prevented important information from being omitted.

Aim: To pilot a selection of indicators in the area of stroke that relate to the care and management of stroke patients in an acute setting.

Source: Hereford Hospitals NHS Trust: Stroke Rehabilitation Service

Authors: Michelle Probert (Nurse Specialist), Peter Overstall (Consultant in Geriatric Medicine)

Stroke rehabilitation service

- Until July 1996, Hereford had no formal rehabilitation programme for stroke patients within the primary or secondary health care settings. A peripatetic stroke team (Stroke Discharge Team [SDT]) was then established with charitable funds.

- The team is led by a nurse (experienced in hospital and community care) and consists of two physiotherapists and an occupational therapist.

- Assessment is initiated early in the acute setting and collaborative care plans operate wherever the patient happens to be in the hospital.

- Discharge is planned with the primary health care team as early as possible.

- Multi-disciplinary therapy continues until the patient reaches their plateau which combined with socio-psychological support by the nurse is the mainstay of care thereafter, which makes the team unique in Herefordshire.

- Only patients who live within a seven mile radius of the hospital are treated by the SDT.

- Patients outside the catchment area have no formal stroke rehabilitation service available to them.

- Patients over 65 years have access to the general rehabilitation ward.

Stroke outcomes pilot study

Period of study:	6 October 1997 to 5 January 1998
Number of patients:	50 patients registered (but 10 incomplete, therefore not used in study; 40 patients complete episodes)
Mean age:	76.85 (minimum 45; maximum 92; Std deviation 10.87)
Male/Female:	Male 52.5%; Female 47.5; (*n* = 40)
Case fatality rate:	30% (*n* = 40)
Stroke discharge team:	Treated 33% of patients (*n* = 40)
Length of stay:	Range = minimum 4 – maximum 109 (*n* = 39); mean – 32.15; Std deviation 27.07
Stroke discharge team	
Length of stay:	Range = minimum 5 – maximum 109; range 104 (*n* = 15); mean length of stay 38.6
Age range:	Minimum 69 – maximum 85; range 16 (*n* = 15); mean age 78.2; Std deviation 4.9

Distribution of Barthel at discharge

- 18/50 Barthel Index recorded on admission
- 0/50 recorded at discharge/transfer to rehabilitation

Issues:

- Estimation of Barthel left to nursing staff
- Lapsed on some wards since infrequently requested by medical staff

Stroke outcomes pilot study

Stroke patients are admitted to a variety of destinations:

- Emergency admission unit (EAU) (opened since completion of study)
- 3 medical wards
- 4 elderly care wards

The study has highlighted some difficulties and the following points should be noted:

1. **Feasibility of data collection**

   All information presently collected by stroke co-ordinator using stroke register.

   Difficulties occur due to:

   - logistically difficult as 2 centre site
   - not all patients admitted to EAU, therefore reliant on ward staff informing co-ordinator of admission
   - co-ordinator not always informed of transfers within hospital especially during bed crisis
   - discharge Barthel difficult to obtain as stroke co-ordinator only involved in discharge planning of stroke discharge team patients.

   During the period of data collection much of the information had to be obtained retrospectively post discharge using medical and nursing notes – this would not be feasible on a long-term basis. Lack of uniformity in the notes also made retrospective data collection difficult, for example, a stroke proforma is used in the medical notes within the Age Care department but not in the EAU or medical wards. Data collection for patients who are treated by the Stroke Discharge Team was more readily available.

2. **Barthel**

   The use of Barthel on discharge as predictor for outcome has little relevance when applied to stroke team patients as the team continue rehabilitation post discharge until the patient plateaus.

3. **Swallow**

   - Swallow test is identified only on the stroke proforma used in the medical notes. Unfortunately, it is not always completed by the physicians which has, at times, made it difficult to record whether the swallow has been assessed – in these cases it has been entered as 'no'. It should also be noted the assessment of swallow by SALT was taken within the first 24 hours – this meant the answer was always 'no' but all patients with identified swallowing difficulties were seen by the SALT.

- No standardised swallow assessment and no clear identification of responsibility, ie nursing/medical potentially led to inter-rater variation.

- On a more positive note, since completion of the study discussions have commenced to ensure reliability and use of standardised stroke proforma across the Trust.

Aim: Pilot of a selection of stroke outcome indicators

Source: Southampton General Hospital, Elderly Care Unit

Authors: Helen Roberts (Consultant Physician), Ibrahim Bodagh (Associate Specialist), Stella Pronk (Senior Occupational Therapist)

Elderly care unit, Southampton General Hospital

Acute stroke admissions patients aged 80+

122 beds/310 stroke patients 1997

Mean length of stay 14 days

6-bed stroke unit

Patients transferred to Consultant rehabilitation beds in community rehabilitation hospitals – Western and Moorgreen – mean length of stay in rehabilitation – 37 days

Patients

50 patients with stroke admitted to the Elderly Care Unit at Southampton General Hospital between November 1997 and March 1998

38 females and 12 males; age range 80–98 years; mean 86 years

51% have left hemiparesis; 36% have right hemiparesis; 13% no clear lateralising signs.

Feasibility of data collection

- Medical staff unreliable at completing audit proforma
- Difficult to add data at admission, 24 hours and 1 week
- Designated audit assistant would have ensured greater recovery of data
- Greater involvement of non-medical staff required
- Incorporation into care pathway for stroke would lead to more data recorded

Percentage of patients with formal swallow assessment with 24 hours

- 9/50 patients had documented Speech and language therapist (SALT) involvement within 24 hours
- 18/50 had SALT involvement within acute unit

Issues:

- Does not capture how many of the remaining patients required SALT or speed of SALT response
- Does not capture dysphagia-trained nurse assessments

Incidence of pressure sores

- 1/50 patients

Issues:

- Requires validation to be reliable
- Collection of incidence of other complications, eg pneumonia, may add face validity especially if 'missing' data

Multi-professional involvement in week 1

- Medical nursing 50/50 patients
- Physiotherapy 24/50
- Occupational therapy 10/50
- SALT 18/50
- Dietitian 11/50

Issues:

- Incomplete recording of data on audit form/medical notes underestimates input
- Multi-disciplinary notes may help
- Requires audit of therapy notes
- Little role for Social Worker/Clinical Psychology in week 1

Distribution of Barthel at discharge

- 18/50 Barthel Index recorded on admission
- 0/50 recorded at discharge/transfer to rehabilitation

Issues:

- Estimation of Barthel left to nursing staff
- Lapsed on some wards since infrequently requested by medical staff

Aim: Measuring clinical outcome in stroke (acute care)

Source: North Staffordshire Combined Healthcare NHS Trust Stroke Service (Acute Beds) and Elderly Care Unit

Authors: Annelies Vreeburg (Specialist Registrar in Geriatric Medicine); Linda Christie (Stroke Co-ordinator); Peter Crome (Professor of Geriatric Medicine, School of Postgraduate Medicine, Keele University); Christine Roffe (Consultant in Stroke Medicine/Senior Lecturer)

Background

- North Staffordshire has a population of about 460,000. Care of the Elderly is provided by the North Staffordshire Combined Healthcare NHS Trust.

- The Geriatric Department of the City General Hospital in Stoke-on-Trent has an Acute Stroke Unit of 10 beds and an Acute Geriatric Assessment Unit of 74 beds.

- There is a 20-bed Stroke Rehabilitation Unit at Bucknall Hospital.

- This pilot study was performed in the Geriatric Department at the City General Hospital.

Positive elements when collecting the data for the pilot study

- Nurses were shown to be good team workers.

- The demographic data were well recorded, there was no problem in collection.

- Systematic classification of the clinical diagnosis gives an insight into the degree of severity of the presenting condition. This has a bearing on the outcome of the acute admission and the prognosis after discharge.

- The project highlighted the logistical difficulties of providing acute diagnostic facilities (eg CT scan).

- The procedure for assessing the patients' ability to swallow safely was not as well implemented as was believed.

- Pressure sores are still a problem.

Difficulties when collecting the data for the pilot study

- Although algorithms and checklists were used, the original reference was not usually mentioned in the forms, and other sources of this information were not readily available.

- All three wards of the Elderly Care Unit had different systems of keeping nursing notes.

- Therapy staff often had separate documentation systems, resulting in under reporting of multi-professional input.

- The stroke patients were managed in different locations which made outcome data on discharge difficult to collect.

Issues:

▌ Collaborative care document in use on one ward made data collection much simpler.

▌ Where the multi-professional documentation system was not in place, a further audit of therapy notes is required to validate data.

Aim: Measuring pressure damage in stroke patients

Source: Guy's and St Thomas' NHS Trust

Authors: Helena Baxter (Clinical Nurse Specialist)

Recommendations

The incidence of pressure damage and the appropriate use of pressure-relieving equipment and nursing strategies in stroke patients is of vital importance, both in terms of patient morbidity/mortality and financial implications.

The pilot study of this project led us to several conclusions:

- Our proforma for pressure damage is quick and easy to complete and should be included as part of the main stroke audit tool, not completed separately.

- Operational definitions need to be made more clear on terms, such as 'documented management plan' in order to improve the audit tool and reduce the risks of poor inter-rater reliability.

- The recording of vital information in separate sections of the notes (eg physiotherapy notes, occupational therapy notes, nursing notes and medical notes) made data gathering difficult and disparate, rather than giving an overall picture of care and achievement of goals.

Overall, the audit was received positively by members of the multi-disciplinary team and provided much food for thought. One of the positive outcomes for the stroke unit has been the piloting of multi-disciplinary notes in an attempt to draw the focus of care back to the patient, rather than the focus being on each disciplines' individual goals.

A multi-disciplinary approach to audit lends itself well to open discussion of care and the examination of each others' roles and approaches to the achievement of patient goals.

8 A summary of the seminar discussion of stroke outcome indicators

David Barer (Professor of Stroke Medicine), Walter W Holland (Emeritus Professor of Public Health Medicine) and Derick Wade (Consultant and Professor in Neurological Disability)

The Stroke Outcomes Seminar, held on 1 July 1998 at the Royal College of Physicians in London, aimed to analyse the results of a pilot project undertaken by the Royal College of Physicians' Clinical Effectiveness and Evaluation Unit (CEEU), and to provide guidance for the future development of outcomes work in this area.

Multi-professional workshop groups (see list of seminar contributors) were assigned to discuss the indicators listed below, in the light of the results of a pilot study carried out among a range of hospitals to test such topics as the feasibility of data collection as well as to provide some illustrative values. The outcome indicators (see Appendix 1 for fuller description) studied were:

- Incidence of pressure sores during the inpatient stay within a hospital provider unit population with a primary diagnosis of stroke.

- Multi-professional involvement in the week following admission within a provider unit population admitted with a primary diagnosis of stroke.

- Distribution of the Barthel Index of Activities of Daily Living (ADL) scores, at discharge from hospital, within a provider unit population with a primary diagnosis of stroke.

- Percentage of patients within a provider unit population for whom a formal swallowing assessment was undertaken within 24 hours of a stroke.

The tasks of the workshop sessions

Each workshop was presented with a series of issues and questions arising from the pilot study:

- Definition of each item and the feasibility of collecting data?

- Reliability of the data collected?

- Variability of the data; reasons, eg poor quality data; clinical variability; casemix considerations etc?

- Applicability of using the indicators. What is the appropriate setting? What caveats should be applied before interpreting the data?

1. Pressure sore incidence

Definition of a pressure sore

The definition of a pressure sore set out in *Effective Health Care Bulletin*[1] on the prevention and treatment of pressure sores, was agreed upon:

> *A new or established area of skin and/or tissue discoloration or damage which persists after the removal of pressure and which is likely to be due to the effects of pressure on the tissues.*

The aim of the indicator was specified in the National Centre for Health Outcomes Development (NCHOD) report as to: '*reduce or avoid complications from stroke*', and its potential uses identified as '*clinical management of patients, clinical audit and provider comparisons*'.[2]

The workshop noted that the indicator on pressure sores does not fulfil the criteria of a *stroke-specific* measure, ie it can and does apply in a wide range of other conditions throughout the hospital.

Various systems have been developed to grade pressure sores, mainly based on clinical presentation (see Table 1, for example). However, the detection and grading of sores, particularly in their very early stages, can be quite subjective and unreliable.[1]

Table 1. Gradations of pressure sores.

Grade 1:	Discoloration of intact skin, including non-blanchable erythema, blue/purple and black discoloration.
Grade 2:	Partial-thickness skin loss or damage involving epidermis and/or dermis.
Grade 3:	Full-thickness skin loss involving damage or necrosis of subcutaneous tissues; but not through the underlying fascia and not extending to the underlying bone, tendon or joint capsule.
Grade 4:	Full-thickness skin loss with extensive destruction, and tissue necrosis extending to the underlying bone, tendon or joint capsule.

It was agreed that pressure sores of grade 2 and above, should be measured in all institutional settings, ie hospital, nursing homes, residential homes, and hospital at home. There should be two measurements recorded:

1   those at risk of developing a pressure sore

2   incidence of grade 2 or greater pressure sores

Incidence or prevalence

Incidence rate:

The rate at which new events occur in a population. The numerator is the number of new events that occur in a defined period, the denominator is the population at risk of experiencing the event during this period.

Prevalence:

The number of instances of a given disease or other condition in a given population at a designated time.[1]

Many professionals and patients believe that pressure sores occur much more frequently than the health service presently recognises, but because definitions and reporting of pressures sores are not standardised, this cannot be confirmed. Pressure sores are preventable if the circumstances that lead to them are identified and preventive policies instituted. It is therefore important that data on the incidence of pressure sores be collected and recorded in a standard way throughout the hospital using a *general standard proforma*. Checking for the development of pressure sores should continue through the period of the hospital stay up to discharge. The existing hospital systems for data collection on pressure sores is variable and was not considered to be generally reliable. The workshop recommended the establishment of a standardised system for all hospitals.

Recording incidence figures was regarded to be a more valid method of recording true level of pressure sores, because it avoids the pitfall of double counting as patients move from one ward or institution to another. Collecting *prevalence* data records what happened at some time in the past, which might have been in a different institution and therefore does not allow for investigation of the causal factors. It is generally recognised that incidence of pressure sores *reflects* on the *quality* of service. In addition, the associated pain and discomfort impacts on patient rehabilitation and progress. Stroke services are in an ideal position to show that measurement of incidence of pressure sores can and should be done.

Collection of data

The management of patients with pressure sores is influenced by the character of the Tissue Viability Management team in each hospital. If a hospital is going to take pressure sore incidence collection seriously they need people – tissue viability nurses – who in addition to their direct patient responsibilities can maintain systems for weekly data collection. Current data systems are unlikely to record all pressure sores. The measurement of incidence requires regular examination of patients and reporting of the observations and is thus dependent on the assiduousness of ward staff and their willingness to comply. It was felt that using tissue viability teams to collect the data would be the most reliable way of collecting incidence data from busy clinical wards although it was recognised that this would mean an increased cost.

To help interpretation of the data, the risk of development of pressure sores should be recorded for each patient admitted with stroke, a responsibility that should be undertaken by the named nurse responsible for the care of the patient.

The recording of incidence data should be possible on all medical units and the response to each occurrence should take place locally within each unit. In addition, there should be awareness and monitoring of the incidence figures by others in the hospital, including management, to ensure that data are being collected to the appropriate standard.

Comparative figures

Comparison of pressure sore incidence between hospitals is fraught with difficulty. It is unclear whether hospitals that report a high incidence of pressure sores are providing poorer care, or simply have a better surveillance system, and/or a lower threshold for reporting a pressure sore. This is an indicator that is vulnerable to data distortions that might occur if comparisons between hospitals were widely publicised, since 'poor' performers could improve their results simply by being less vigilant in reporting, or by raising the threshold for what is defined as a pressure sore.

The incidence figures recorded in the pilot study were small, ranging from 0% to 7% in different units. This makes it statistically impossible to compare occurrence rates between units over periods even as long as a year, and also difficult to analyse longitudinal data within a unit over a few years simply because the numbers are too low for statistical significance to be attained. To detect a change in incidence from 2% to 4% with 80% power and 95% confidence would need 1,240 patients in each hospital/time period. Such numbers would be feasible if all patients in a hospital were to be included and not just stroke cases, but the further adjustments needed for casemix, severity of illness, for diagnosis, age and length of stay would make sensible interpretation almost impossible. Recent experience of coding in routine information systems suggests that the quality of the data is not yet sufficient to allow this to be performed accurately.[3]

Every organisation should record the incidence of new pressure sores arising in stroke patients. The incidence rates should be used only as an indicator of the quality of preventive care if the patients' risk of developing a sore is taken into account. The group did not specify which risk factors should be recorded.

Critical incident analysis

Although the overall incidence of pressure sores is relatively low, they are still sufficiently common in both hospital and community settings, to represent a significant burden of suffering for patients and their carers and be very costly to the NHS.

It is possible to treat the occurrence of a pressure sore as a *critical incident* worthy of specific investigation. A pressure sore is an example of an adverse event – an incident that under optimal conditions is not a normal consequence of a patient's disease or treatment. As an avoidable complication it should be investigated with the aim of establishing how and why it occurred. Results of the investigation need to be fed back directly to the staff on the unit so that necessary remedial action can be taken.

Commissioners of health care could specify in service agreements that hospitals should have in place systems to detect and investigate the occurrence of pressure sores and ask for evidence that lessons learnt had influenced clinical policy and practice to reduce incidence in future. Hospitals with high incidence figures in succeeding years should have their systems questioned. Trust managers should regard pressure sore prevention as a risk management issue and both management and professionals should be involved in the interpretation of, and response to, survey and audit data on pressure sores.

Applicability

The workshop accepted that a high incidence of pressure sores is a possible indicator of poor quality of care. It is therefore reasonable to specify pressure sore incidence as a quality measure in all corporate contracts, ie contracting and regulatory units of care and nursing homes. This would require a corporate responsibility not only to measure the incidence, ie of grade 2 pressure sores or greater, but also to designate responsibility to an appropriate person within each Trust or responsible authority to collect the data and ensure appropriate investigation of each occurrence. It will be necessary to ensure that not only are there systems for recording pressure sore incidence data, but also the 'risks' for each patient admitted which may need separate mechanisms. Both factors need to be recorded if the data are to be interpretable.

The systems set up must apply to all institutions caring for stroke patients. It was noted that contracts with nursing homes for accommodation may be provided by social services but that the quality of health care, and inspection of nursing and medical standards should remain a duty carried out by Health Authorities. The same critical incident approach is applicable in all types of institution.

Finally the workshop noted that it was not sufficient merely to count the incidence figures but there should also be an effective policy for the treatment of pressure sores (which should be modelled on the *Effective Health Care* bulletin[1]) in each hospital, nursing home and residential care home.

2.   Multi-professional involvement in the case of stroke patients

The rationale for using this outcome indicator is that well organised multi-disciplinary rehabilitation increases the rate of improvement in stroke patients, although its long-term effectiveness is unclear.[4] Stroke patients managed within specialist units (where a key characteristic was specialist multi-disciplinary team care) are more likely to be alive and living at home a year after stroke, than those patients managed under general medical wards.[4,5] While this indicator measures the level of multi-professional input within stroke care, it should be recognised that this may reflect the availability of necessary resources as much as it reflects on the organisation of care.

Definition

The workshop noted that it is difficult to define a multi-disciplinary team. Every in-patient will be seen by a doctor and a nurse, but the questions are: how many other professions should be included in order to define care as multi-disciplinary? Should specific professions be named? What degree of specialisation is required? And how is this defined? If a clear working definition is missing there is the danger that the indicator could be used for comparison between different institutions, leading to the development of different standards of care.

It was felt important to recognise that the competency of various professions varied not only with the qualification but also with their specific knowledge and experience of stroke care. To improve care of patients with stroke there is a need for people who are *experts* in stroke rather than *those who only have an interest in it.*

A multi-disciplinary team for stroke patients should equal at least three professionals who have a dedicated interest and expertise in the co-ordinated care and management of stroke. There needs to be written evidence in the medical notes of collaborative goal planning between members of the team. This would serve as working evidence of multi-disciplinary involvement. The workshop recommended that the definition of a multi-disciplinary team should appear in an appropriate healthcare bulletin. Furthermore, community care plans should require Health Authorities to move towards dedicated teams which include social workers. This means it should be a cross boundary contract.

Issues of reliability and variability

The workshop noted that efforts to implement this indicator will need to take into account the extra work required for its collection, noting that this could overburden many stroke services which are already thinly resourced and overstretched. There is also the danger of generating a *perverse incentive* whereby patients are kept in longer than they may need so as to fulfil quotas of multi-professional involvement.

The workshop outlined the following key aspects of the indicator necessary to make it truly measure multi-professional involvement:

- An identifiable set of team notes so that there is a unitary record for all patients with stroke in which matters are recorded by doctors, nurses, physiotherapists etc. This avoids the duplication of examinations and testing that occurs at present.

- Evidence of team meetings about individual patients within seven days of stroke.

- Ascertaining whether or not the treatment of an individual patient is appropriate and co-ordinated by a multi-professional team.

In all cases it is important that there be a note both of the numerator and of the denominator so that the set of team notes is not only used for patients on a stroke ward but for all stroke patients in the whole hospital.

Applicability

Targets based upon this indicator could be used by both Trust management and commissioners. Failure to meet a target could provide a case for increased resources. Commissioners would need evidence that reorganising existing services would achieve the targets. From the strategic point of view, it is likely that access to multi-disciplinary care would form an important part of a local health improvement programme for stroke.

The measurement of multi-professional involvement should be carried out on the basis of each of the individual professions. There needs to be a measure of whether the team had regular meetings as a body, along with evidence that the patients were both seen and discussed by one or more members of the team. This measure should be used periodically and it should record the proportion of patients treated by the team.

3. Distribution of Barthel Index of Activities of Daily Living

The aim of recording Barthel scores is to improve function and well-being after stroke. Its potential uses are for clinical audit and provider-based comparisons for clinicians, commissioners and provider management. Stroke is a major cause of functional impairment. Rehabilitation following stroke aims to minimise disability and handicap. Assessment of functional ability to evaluate the resulting impact of rehabilitation services may be a useful indicator of successful care. Measurement of the functional status of patients at discharge will in part reflect the effectiveness of stroke management and rehabilitation. In addition, this indicator provides a baseline for longitudinal follow-up of patients' functioning.

The workshop noted that one of the published sets of guidelines for the Barthel should be recommended for use as the best definition for the individual items.

Table 2. Barthel ADL Functional Assessment Scale.

Bowels
0 = incontinent (or needs to be given enemata)
1 = occasional accident (one/week)
2 = continent

Mobility
0 = immobile
1 = wheel chair independent including corners etc
2 = walks with help of one person (verbal or physical)
3 = independent (may use stick etc)

Bladder
0 = incontinent, or catheterised
1 = occasional accident (max once per 24 hours)
2 = continent (over 7 days)

Transfer
0 = unable - no sitting balance
1 = major help (one/two people) can sit
2 = minor help (verbal or physical)
3 = independent

Grooming
0 = needs help with personal care
1 = independent face/hair/teeth/shaving
   (implements provided)

Dressing
0 = dependent
1 = needs help, can do half unaided
2 = independent (including buttons, zips, laces etc)

Toilet use
0 = dependent
1 = needs some help, can do something alone
2 = independent (on and off, dressing/wiping)

Stairs
0 = unable
1 = needs help (verbal/physical)
2 = independent

Feeding
0 = unable
1 = needs help cutting, etc
2 = independent (food in reach)

Bathing
0 = dependent
1 = independent

Issues of reliability and variability

The source of the information should be the best available source. This would be achieved by including it within Trust discharge policies.

Routine collection of Barthel ADL index at discharge would have several uses. It could be used by hospital management either to identify cases where length of stay was longer than expected, or in situations where length of stay was shorter, leading to early discharge. This would require adjustment for casemix in order to identify specific problems that result in delayed discharge – particularly relevant in acute hospital settings where bed availability is at a premium. Health care professionals could also use it to ensure that specific problems relating to disability of individual patients have been identified, and that a treatment plan has been formulated to address these needs after discharge.

The workshop agreed that the reporting currency should be the 10 item/20 point Barthel ADL index. The preferred time of measurement should be at the point of transfer from secondary to primary care. The preference is to also record it at six months post stroke. The data should be collected prospectively, rather than retrospectively and should be used in the context of other information on length of stay, discharge destination, pre-morbid function, initial severity of stroke and type of services involved.

The workshop also noted that the data for Barthel ADL are very difficult to interpret and most professionals had goals that lay outside achieving simple independence in ADL. These include maximising social functioning and reducing carer and patient distress. Small differences in Barthel scores may be explained by confounding factors. It is large differences that are more likely to be significant.

The workshop felt that it would be quite appropriate to collect the extended Barthel score or to use another commensurate system of measurement. Established (and validated) mathematical calculations exist which allow conversion to a standard Barthel score from other more complex scores.

The workshop emphasised that if Barthel ADL index was to be used there is a need for proper information systems along with appropriate training provided to ensure agreement on *who is performing the measurement*, and *what the words mean*.

Applicability

The Barthel ADL index is a true measure of outcome, albeit with the already noted problems about interpretation. It should be used by the local service to help analyse its own performance, but it should not be used to compare services. Many patients are transferred one or more times while in secondary care (ie from acute ward to a rehabilitation setting and then possibly to a community hospital) prior to discharge. A number of elements need to be taken into account before interpretation:

1. The type of unit involved and whether the unit would be aiming towards improving emotional status and not just outcome, social functioning, outdoor mobility, communication and carer stress.

2. Although the unit may turn out to be judged on the Barthel by others, it should judge its own success and put significant resources into many other outcomes of importance.

3. There needs to be a formal recognition that although Barthel measurement was feasible, practical and does reflect health input, it did not encompass all that healthcare was trying to achieve. There are a number of dimensions to health care improvement, beyond those recorded by the Barthel measurement.

Barthel scores should be used as an indicator of the overall organisation and performance of the totality of stroke services organised and bought by the commissioner, and not primarily as an indicator of a single unit.

There should also be an additional component, not in place of Barthel, which includes some assessment of psychological or emotional outcome. This was certainly important to the patient and maybe one of the major determinants from their point of view. One possible way of doing this would be to use the additional question: *'do you feel sad and depressed?'*

4. Swallowing assessment

The aim of the indicator is to reduce or avoid complication of stroke. Its potential uses are for clinical audit and management of patients.

Formal swallowing assessment is a process measure that is specific to acute stroke. It is an indicator of a high quality of service, that points to an awareness of specific stroke problems and an ability to organise care routinely.

There were two possible ways in which this indicator might be defined. The first very simple approach is to look for any evidence in the medical notes of a mention of swallowing, or where swallowing had been considered or thought about. Such an approach would include virtually any mention of swallowing without stipulating any criteria about the nature of the assessment, whether it was a full assessment by speech and language therapists, or by a doctor checking the gag reflex or something of that kind. The second, and preferred approach is an assessment based on an agreed upon inter-disciplinary protocol or assessment pathway, recognising that not all stroke patients need to have the same type of assessment. Obviously unconscious patients would not do a formal water swallowing test. The assessment should be done by an appropriately trained person, a doctor or a nurse, most likely a nurse rather than a speech and language therapist because the issue is dysphagia screening rather than full assessment.

The workshop agreed that the definition of proper swallowing assessment must involve some kind of assessment pathway because not all patients are appropriate for a formal bedside swallowing test. The figures could be collected on a routine or periodic basis but only if the proper building blocks are in place. There needs to be a hospital policy in place and training provided. Without either of these preconditions the figures are not going to be very meaningful.

Issues of reliability and variability

It may be necessary before recommending swallowing assessment as an outcome or process measure, that a period of time be devoted to disseminating guidelines on dysphagia management. This would allow hospitals a chance to prepare to collect these data.

The workshop suggested that the information should not be collected by the same person who is recording the swallowing assessment. Data collection should be the responsibility of the audit department possibly on a one off basis for a month's worth of stroke admissions or 25 patients, whichever one is the lesser.

There are serious concerns about comparative figures being available for swallowing assessments because the interpretation can vary dramatically in different units. If the information is being used in-house as a starting point for getting a proper management policy off the ground, it would have value. However, if it is to be used as a public health type measure for general comparison it could lead to *perverse incentives*.

The workshop noted that there could be many interpretations of what constitutes a valid assessment. In the absence of clear evidence, local policies are likely to vary. The workshop concluded that a simple definition should be: *every patient should have their swallowing assessed formally using an agreed, standardised assessment protocol undertaken by a suitably trained professional, and that this should be recorded in the notes.*

Testing the gag reflex was not an assessment of swallowing. As a minimum there should be a note of swallowing safety followed by an indication of swallowing management (unless the patient is unconscious or another valid reason for not assessing the patient is stated).

Applicability

Comparison with results elsewhere would inform debate on what appropriate targets might be set:

- For health care professionals, such targets could form the focus for training junior staff by raising awareness of an important problem that is often overlooked and not recorded in the medical or nursing notes.

- For Trust management, appropriate assessment and management of swallowing is an important risk management issue, since dysphagia is associated with aspiration pneumonia.

- From the point of view of commissioners in Primary Health Care Groups and Health Authorities, measurable targets could be set in contracts with Trusts to reflect local policy.

The workshop expressed a number of ideas for structural measures which could help the implementation and reliability of this indicator. They included the recommendation that each hospital should develop an appropriate inter-disciplinary dysphagia management policy and a training programme for appropriate staff. Once these conditions have been fulfilled, there would then be a second stage which would involve the development of a more sophisticated tool which measured the proportion of patients who are assessed by someone with appropriate training in dysphagia screening according to an agreed policy and carried out before the first oral intake up to a maximum of 24-hours after admission.

Summary points

- The seminar concluded with broad agreement that the four pilot indicators were each worth collecting.

- If used carefully the data should help to improve stroke management.

- Two items (pressure sores and Barthel ADL) were recommended for routine collection in every unit.

- Two items (multi-professional involvement and swallowing assessment) were recommended for periodic collection, eg for a month every year or two.

- The seminar also agreed that the other outcome indicator (not piloted in this study) that should be measured is the patient's feeling of well-being (ie, their emotional state).

References

1. Effective Health Care. *The prevention and treatment of pressure sores.* Leeds: Nuffield Institute for Health, University of Leeds, NHS Centre for Reviews and Dissemination, University of York, 1995.

2. Rudd A, Goldacre M, Amess M, Fletcher J *et al* (eds). *Health Outcome Indicators: Stroke. Report of a working group to the Department of Health.* Oxford: National Centre for Health Outcomes Development, 1999.

3.   Mant J, Mant F, Winner S. How good is routine information? Validation of coding for acute stroke in Oxford hospitals. *Health Trends* 1997/98; **28**: 96-99.

4.   Stroke Unit Trialists Collaboration. Collaborative systematic review of the randomised trials of organised inpatient (stroke unit) care after stroke. *Br Med J* 1997; **314**: 1151-1159.

5.   Stroke Unit Trialists Collaboration. How do stroke units improve patient outcomes? A collaborative systematic review of the randomised trials. *Stroke* 1997; **28**: 2139-2144.

Candidate indicators

Reprinted from Rudd A, Goldacre M, Amess M, Fletcher J *et al* (eds). *Health outcome indicators: Stroke. Report of a working group to the Department of Health.* Oxford: National Centre for Health Outcomes Development, 1999.

Candidate indicator 9

Title

Percentage of patients within a provider unit population for whom a formal swallowing assessment was undertaken within 24 hours of a stroke

Aim of health intervention

Reduce or avoid complications of stroke.

Characteristics
Specificity: Condition-specific
Perspective: Clinical
Timeframe: Cross-sectional
Outcome relationship: Indirect

Definition

For a given provider unit population and year: *the number of patients for whom a formal swallowing assessment was undertaken and documented, within 24 hours of admission for a stroke in the given year, divided by the number of patients admitted for stroke within the relevant year.* The resulting fraction should be expressed as a percentage and reported in patient age-groups.

Rationale

Dysphagia has been reported to occur in 28–45% of patients with acute stroke.[1] Aspiration has been found in 32–51% of patients with stroke and dysphagia.[2–4] Pneumonia is a complication of aspiration,[4] and is also the second most frequent cause of death within the first month after cerebral infarction, accounting for nearly one-third of stroke deaths.[5] An immediate assessment of swallowing is important in treating patients with acute stroke. Careful assessment and management of dysphagia may dramatically reduce aspiration complications and the associated increased length of stay.[6]

Potential uses

Clinical audit; management of patients.

Potential users

Clinicians; provider managers; commissioners.

Possible confounders

No specific confounders identified.

Data sources

Currently, collection of numerator data would require a survey of patient notes to identify whether an assessment has been made, ie a note of such or by the presence of an assessment form, eg the standardised bedside swallowing assessment (SSA). Alternatively, where more sophisticated clinical information systems including multi-professional patient records are available, the data may be more accessible and their analysis more feasible on a routine basis.

Data quality

The quality of the data would rely on the legibility and completeness of patient documentation, which will vary. A dedicated field within a computerised system would increase the reliability and completeness of such data.

Comments

The relationship between the assessment and treatment of dysphagia has not been fully investigated in terms of outcomes of death or avoidable chest infections. It is recognised that dysphagia is common and associated with a worse outcome,[4] but this may simply be that dysphagia accompanies severe strokes and therefore interventions to reduce swallowing problems may not affect morbidity or mortality. In the future, measuring of the occurrence of chest infections alongside this indicator may be valuable.

Further work

Investigation of the reliability of surveys to collect swallowing assessment data from patient notes, and further research to establish whether the identification of dysphagia leads to reduction in mortality and morbidity.

Conclusions and priority

Priority E. To be further developed because link with effectiveness is not clear.

References

1. Odderson IR, McKenna BS. A model for management of patients with stroke during the acute phase, outcome and economic implications. *Stroke* 1993; **24**: 1823–7.

2. Barer DH. Lower cranial motor function in unilateral vascular lesions of the cerebral hemisphere. *Br Med J* 1984; **289**: 1621–2.

3. Barer DH. The natural history and functional consequences of dysphagia after hemispheric stroke. *J Neurol Neurosurg Psychiatry* 1989; **52**: 236–41.

4. Gordon C, Langton-Hewer RL, Wade DT. Dysphagia in acute stroke. *Br Med J* 1987; **295**: 411–4.

5. Bounds JV, Wiebers DO, Whisant JP, Okazaki H. Mechanisms and timing of deaths from cerebral infarction. *Stroke* 1981; **12**: 474–7.

6. Odderson IR, Keaton JC, McKenna BS. Swallow management in patients on an acute stroke pathway: quality is cost effective. *Arch Phys Med Rehabil* 1995; **76**: 1130–3.

Candidate indicator 10

Title

Incidence of pressure sores during the in-patient stay within a hospital provider unit population with a primary diagnosis of stroke

Aim of health intervention

Reduce or avoid complications from stroke.

Characteristics

Specificity: Generic
Perspective: Clinical
Timeframe: Cross-sectional
Outcome relationship: Direct

Definition

For a given provider unit population and year: *the number of patients admitted with a stroke who acquire one or more pressure sores during a hospital provider spell which ends in the given year, divided by the total number of patients admitted with a stroke who were discharged in the given year.* For the purpose of this indicator, only pressure sores of grade 2 or above should be counted. The resulting fraction should be expressed as a percentage and reported as an overall figure and by age-group and sex.

Rationale

Pressure sores are common in hospital settings, represent a significant burden on patients and their carers, and are costly to the NHS.[1] New pressure sores occurred in 4–10% of patients admitted to a UK district general hospital, depending on the case-mix.[2] Health authorities received guidance from the NHS Management Executive encouraging them to set targets for an overall reduction in prevalence of at least 5%.[3] Evidence and experience suggest, however, that prevalence rates, because they are affected by incidence rates, healing rates, admission and discharge policies, are very difficult to interpret.[1] Comparisons of incidence rates are therefore proposed but will only reflect the effect of prevention policies if suitable adjustment is made for differences in risk status of patients admitted.[1]

The indicator is specified as the incidence of acquired pressure sores of grade 2 and above so as to avoid the difficulties of reliable assessment of grade 1 pressure sores, consisting of non-blanchable erythema with intact skin.

Potential uses

Clinical audit; management of patients; provider comparisons.

Potential users

Clinicians; commissioners; provider management.

Possible confounders

To control for relevant patient risk factors, the indicator data should ideally be analysed per 'at risk' group.

Data sources

Many provider units are monitoring pressure sore rates, most by weekly data collection of assessment proformas completed by ward staff or, where facilities are in place, entering them onto a ward nursing system alongside other patients' details. Whether a paper or computerised data collection system is in place, the minimum information required would be: patient's identification details, patient diagnosis, and an assessment of pressure sore status on admission (to identify pressure sores acquired during the inpatient stay). Several pressure sore grading systems are in use nationally,[4] however, four ulcer stages are generally used.[5] To allow data comparison, grading systems that define a grade/stage 2 pressure sore as 'partial thickness skin loss or damage involving epidermis and/or dermis'[5] should be used. This staging is from an ulcer scale developed and generally used for reporting the prevalence of pressure sores, and guiding therapy.[6]

Currently, retrospective monitoring of CMDS data would allow identification of pressure sores (Decubitus ulcer, ICD-10 code L89) in patients who also had a primary diagnosis of stroke (ICD-10 codes 161-164) for any episode within any hospital spell. This would allow calculation of *prevalence* rates; ICD-10 coding does not identify *acquired* sores or the grading of sores. The introduction of an additional subdivision of L89 would allow this discrimination. Optional use of Read codes would allow some additional information to be recorded in relation to grade of sore, but at this stage these codes are still under development.

Data quality

The quality of the data would depend on the system in place and on the existence of quality control checks on data entry. The data quality may also be affected by poor inter-rater reliability. This may be addressed by suitable training for all ward staff in the use of both risk and pressure sore assessment tools.

Comments

The *prevalence* of pressure sores can be recorded now in line with the NHS Executive targets. An adjustment to current clinical coding would allow *newly acquired* pressure sores to be recorded. Supporting information on the risk factors of individuals with pressure sores would require more sophisticated systems.

Further work

An additional code to distinguish acquired pressure sores within the ICD-10 coding structure is recommended. To aid interpretation, the development of 'at risk' assessment tools such as the Waterlow or Norton scales should be undertaken.[7]

Conclusion and Priority

Priority A. To be implemented generally on a routine basis.

References

1. Effective Health Care. *The prevention and treatment of pressure sores.* University of Leeds, University of York, 1995.

2. Clark M, Watts S. The incidence of pressure sores within a National Health Service trust hospital during 1991. *J Adv Nurs* 1994; **20**: 33–6.

3. NHS Management Executive. *Priorities and planning guidance 1994–95. EL(93)54.* Leeds: Department of Health, 1993.

4. Healey F. Using incidence data to improve risk assessment. *J Tissue Viability* 1996; **6**: 3–9.

5. Smith DM. Pressure ulcers in the nursing home. *Ann Intern Med* 1995; **123**: 433–42.

6. National Pressure Ulcer Advisory Panel. Pressure ulcer prevalence, cost and risk assessment: consensus statement. *Decubitus* 1989; **2**: 24–8.

7. Smith I. Waterlow/Norton scoring system: a ward view. *CARE-Science and Practice* 1989; **7**: 93–5.

Candidate indicator 13

Title   Multi-professional involvement in the week following admission within a provider unit population admitted with a primary diagnosis of stroke

Aim of health intervention

Improve function and well-being after stroke.

Characteristics

Specificity: Condition-specific

Perspective: Clinical

Timeframe: Cross-sectional

Outcome relationship: Direct

Definition

For a given provider unit and year: *the proportions of patients admitted for stroke in the given year who are assessed within 1 week of admission by each of a set of potentially relevant professions.* The categorisation of professions (shown below) is taken from the Royal College of Physicians Stroke Minimum Data Set proforma. Use of this categorisation would be used to present nine percentage scores.

Which professionals assessed the patient during the first week of admission?

1.	Doctor	6.	Speech and language therapist
2.	Nurse	7.	Clinical psychologist
3.	Physiotherapist	8.	Social worker
4.	Occupational therapist	9.	Other
5.	Dietitian		

Rationale

Well organised multi-disciplinary rehabilitation increases the rate of improvement in stroke patients, although the long-term effectiveness is unclear.[1] Stroke patients managed within specialist units (where a key characteristic was specialist multi-disciplinary team care) compared with general medical wards were more likely to be alive and at home a year after stroke.[2] This indicator will measure the level of multi-professional input within stroke care. It is recognised, however, that this may reflect the availability of necessary resources as much as it reflects on the organisation of the care.

Potential uses

Clinical audit; management of patients.

Potential users

Clinicians; commissioners.

Possible confounders

No specific confounders identified.

Data sources

The numerator information may be obtained from a survey of the notes (probably nursing notes in combination with medical notes) to identify a documented reference to an assessment made by each profession, using the list as the survey tool. Alternatively, this information will be available if used routinely within the Royal College of Physicians Stroke Minimum Data Set. This is a two-sided proforma designed to collect a set of information on each patient admitted with a stroke. Question 12 asks the healthcare staff to tick which of nine types of professionals have assessed the patient during the first week of the admission. Use of this indicator could advance data collection standards. The denominator data may be obtained from CMDS data with a primary diagnosis of stroke for an admission episode (ICD-10 codes I61, I62, I63, I64).

Data quality

The quality of the data may rely on the patient notes or the quality of CMDS data, which are not uniformly reliable. The RCP Stroke Minimum Data Set is about to undergo a formal large-scale pilot.

Comments

As well as presenting the scores as nine separate percentages, other, composite, scores could be used, eg 'percentage of patients assessed by three or more professional groups'. As specified, the indicator captures the range of professional involvement in a given case. Ideally, however, multi-professional care additionally implies co-operation between the professionals. An indicator reflecting the extent to which the individuals work as a multi-professional team would be valuable, but the difficulty of defining an operational measure of this co-operation has led to the more limited approach as specified here.

Further work

None recommended.

Conclusions and priority

Priority B. To be implemented generally by periodic survey.

References

1. Effective Health Care. *The prevention and treatment of pressure sores.* Leeds: University of Leeds, 1995.

2. Stroke Unit Trialists' Collaboration. A systematic review of specialist multi-disciplinary team (stroke unit) care for stroke in patients. In: *The Cochrane Database of Systematic Reviews: Stroke Module* (ed. Warlow C, Van Gijn J, Sandercock P). BMJ Publishing Group, 1995.

Candidate indicator 14

Title   Distribution of the Barthel Index of Activities of Daily Living (ADL), at discharge from hospital, within a provider unit population with a primary diagnosis of stroke

Characteristics

Specificity: Condition-specific
Perspective: Clinical
Timeframe: Cross-sectional
Outcome relationship: Direct

Aim of health intervention

Improve function and well-being after stroke.

Definition

For a given provider unit and year: *a summary of the distribution of Barthel ADL scores, as assessed at discharge, of patients who, having been admitted for stroke, were discharged in the given year.* The indicator should be reported by patient age-band and sex as well as for the whole population. The size of the relevant population together with the number of cases for which an assessment was available should also be reported.

A suitable summary of the distribution would include a measure of both central tendency and dispersion. Both means (and standard deviations) and medians (and interquartile ranges) are used widely in the literature. Alternatively, the distribution could be summarised by using categories such as those suggested by Stone *et al.*[1]

- Independent (Barthel 20)
- Mild dependence (Barthel 15–19)
- Moderate dependence (Barthel 10–14)
- Severe dependence (Barthel 5–9)
- Very severe dependence (Barthel 0–4)

While the total Barthel score provides an assessment of overall disability, it would also be valuable to know about the underlying pattern of specific disabilities. In view of this, the distribution of scores for the individual component items of the Barthel should also be reported.

Rationale

Stroke is a major cause of functional impairment. Rehabilitation following stroke aims to minimise disability and handicap. Assessment of functional ability to evaluate the resulting impact of rehabilitation services may be a useful indicator of successful care. Measurement of the functional status of patients at discharge will in part reflect the effectiveness of stroke management and rehabilitation. In addition, this indicator provides a baseline for longitudinal follow-up of patients' functioning.

Potential uses

Clinical audit; provider-based comparisons.

Potential users

Clinicians; commissioners; provider management.

Possible confounders

Comparisons between populations should be made in the context of casemix information covering severity, co-morbidity and length of stay.

Data sources

The assessment could be made by ward staff and documented in patient notes. To facilitate aggregation of individual assessments, the information could form part of a stroke database. The Royal College of Physicians Stroke Minimum Data Set includes the Barthel Index. When there are practical difficulties in performing a full

Barthel assessment at the time of discharge, it has been shown that the total Barthel score can be accurately predicted from the scores on three easily remembered items: mobility, bed transfers and urinary continence.[2]

Data quality

The Barthel Index has been shown to be reliable with different observers in a wide variety of situations,[3] and it is a valid measure of physical disability.[4] The value of the indicator would be compromised by low rates of completion, which is a danger where the data are not derived from information systems that support operational activities.

Comments

The working group suggested that additional useful information may be obtained if the dimensions assessing 'Bowels' and 'Bladder' are augmented. If the assessment score is 0 in terms of their dependency within these two sections, an additional question as to whether faecal soiling is present could be added for the 'Bowels' subsection, and an additional question to identify those who are 'catheterised' and those who are 'incontinent' for the 'Bladder' section. Inclusion of this additional information does not affect the calculation of the total Barthel score.

A pre-morbid assessment of function is essential to assess the true benefits of the care received. Information currently recorded is often unreliable[5] and could be improved by using standardised assessments such as the Barthel, though this information may be difficult to verify. Where only limited information is available, a hierarchical version of the Barthel Index may be used to estimate the total score.[6]

Further work

Further refinements to augment the index as noted above.

Conclusions and priority

Priority A. To be implemented generally on a routine basis.

References

1. Stone SP, Ali B, Auberleek I, Thompsell A *et al.* The Barthel Index in clinical practice: use on a rehabilitation ward for elderly people. *J R Coll Physicians Lond* 1994; **28**: 419–23.

2. Ellul J, Watkins C, Barer D. Estimating total Barthel scores from just three items: The European Stroke Database minimum dataset for assessing functional status at discharge from hospital. In press.

3. Gompertz P, Pound P, Ebrahim S. The reliability of stroke outcome measures. *Clin Rehabil* 1993; 7: 290–6.

4. Wade DT, Langton-Hewer RL. Functional abilities after stroke: measurement, natural history and prognosis. *J Neurol Neurosurg Psychiatry* 1987; **50**: 177–82.

5. Benbow SJ, Watkins C, Sangster G, Ellul J *et al.* The availability and reliability of information on the pre-morbid functional status of stroke patients in hospital. *Clin Rehabil* 1994; **8**: 281–5.

6. Barer D, Murphy J. Scaling the Barthel: a 10-point hierarchical version of the activities of daily living index for use with stroke patients. *Clin Rehabil* 1993; 7: 221–7.

Glossary

Activities of Daily Living

This term refers to measures of independence in the performance of five major personal care activities, bathing, dressing, eating, getting in and out of bed, using the toilet. Assessment of impairment of physical function is often undertaken using scales constructed from the five activities of daily living (Patrick DL, Erickson P. *Health status and health policy*. Oxford: Oxford University Press, 1993).

Acute

Referring to a brief, not chronic, intense but short-term exposure.

Audit

An audit is an official examination, usually of accounts, to assess how well a business or service is functioning. Auditing is now usually thought of in terms of a cycle whereby practice is assessed by independent observers and checked against prospectively set standards. Any deficiency is highlighted and brought to the attention of the appropriate managers so that appropriate changes can be agreed upon and implemented. Subsequently, practice is again observed to complete the cycle. High standards of practice can therefore be achieved and maintained through this system of quality assurance.

Bias

Bias is the deviation from the truth, due to systematic error(s) in the methods used. There are many different types of bias.

Bias: detection

Detection bias is a difference between the experimental and control group in how the outcomes are measured or diagnosed.

Bias: measurement

Measurement bias occurs when the individual measurements or classifications of disease or exposure are inaccurate, ie they do not measure correctly what they are supposed to measure. This can sometimes be due to biochemical or physiological measurements, which are never completely accurate; laboratories producing systematically different results; or human error.

Bias: observer

Observer bias can occur in the following circumstances: variation due to differences among observers; or variation in readings by the same observer on separate occasions; or when data are analysed by investigators who are aware of the intervention received by the participant. Their analysis can be subconsciously influenced by their knowledge of which treatment was undertaken.

Bias: performance

Due to differences in care provided to treatment or control group other than the intervention that the study is interested in. Measurement bias and responder bias are two types of performance bias.

Case fatality rate

This is the rate for deaths in patients with a particular disease, usually expressed as a percentage: (deaths attributed to the disease, divided by number of cases of the disease) × 100.

Casemix

The mix of types of patient or treatment episode.

Chi-squared (χ^2)

A test statistic used to assess the statistical significance of a finding, based on the difference between the observed frequency of an event and the frequency that would be expected if the null hypothesis were true.

Clinical audit

The systematic and critical analysis of the quality of clinical care, including the procedures used for the diagnosis, treatment and care, the associated use of resources and the resulting outcome and quality of life for the patient or client.

Clinical effectiveness

The extent to which specific clinical interventions, when deployed in the field for a particular patient or population, do what they are intended to do, ie maintain and improve health and secure the greatest possible gain from the available resources.

Clinical governance

A national framework through which NHS organisations are accountable for continuously improving the quality and clinical effectiveness of their services.

Clinical guidelines

Protocols for treatment of a particular condition, disease or trauma, based on the evidence obtained from systematic review of the literature.

Clinicians

Those directly involved in the care and treatment of patients, including doctors, dentists, nurses, midwives, health visitors, pharmacists, opticians, orthoptists, chiropodists, radiographers, physiotherapists, dietitians, occupational therapists, medical laboratory scientific officers, orthotists and prosthetists, therapists, speech and language therapists, and all other healthcare professionals.

Community NHS Trusts

NHS organisations that provide community-based services, chiefly to elderly people, children and people with disabilities. They include district nurses, health visitors, physiotherapists, chiropodists.

Confidence interval (CI)

A sample of people in a trial can be used in order to estimate characteristics of the underlying population. Because estimates vary from sample to sample, it is important to know how close the estimate derived from any one sample is likely to be to the value for the underlying population. One way to find this out is to construct a confidence interval around the estimate, ie construct around the estimate a range of values that have a specified probability of including the true population values. People often speak of a '95% confidence interval' (or '95% confidence limits'). This is the interval that includes the true value in 95% of cases. The size of the confidence interval is related to the size of the sample; larger samples give narrower confidence limits.

Confounder

A variable associated with the exposure under study, and in its own right a risk factor for the disease.

Cross-sectional study

A cross-sectional (or prevalence) study is one in which information is collected in a planned way in a defined population at one point in time. A survey is an example.

Diagnosis

The identification of a disease from its signs and symptoms.

Electronic Health Record (EHR)

The term EHR is used to describe the concept of a longitudinal record of a patient's health and healthcare, from cradle to grave. It combines both information about patient contacts with primary healthcare as well as subsets of information associated with episodic elements of care held in EPRs.

Electronic Patient Record (EPR)

A record containing a patient's personal details (name, date of birth etc), diagnosis or condition, and details about the treatment/assessments undertaken by a clinician. Typically it covers the episodic care provided mainly by one institution.

Feasibility study

A preliminary 'proof-of-concept' evaluation.

Follow-up

Getting results from the participants of a trial all the way through a study period. Losing patients from follow-up can distort the results.

Gold standard

This term in measurement scale development or pharmacoeconomic evaluation refers to the comparator that is generally regarded to be the best available. For example, in the survey of health status, the SF-36 form is often regarded as the gold standard. Therefore, when developing or proposing a new form, it is expected that any validation would include the concurrent use of SF-36.

Hawthorne effect

Psychological response in which subjects change their behaviour simply because they are participants in a study, not because of the research treatment.

Hypothesis

An assumption made as a starting point for further investigation from known facts.

Ideal indicator

What should be known, and realistically could be known, about outcomes relevant to the disease in question.

Incidence

The number of new cases of a disease, or of any other outcome, that develop in a population of individuals at risk during a specified time period.

Indicator

An aggregated statistical measure describing a group or whole population, compiled from measures on individuals, which provide insights about the functioning of services.

Instrument

Technology employed to make a measurement, such as a paper questionnaire. The instrument encodes and embodies the procedures used to determine the presence, absence, or extent of an attribute in an object.

International Classification of Diseases (ICD)

This is a system of disease classification that is regularly updated by the World Health Organization. The classification has its roots in the standard nomenclature for causes of death first proposed by W Farr (1807–83). The latest revision is the 10th (ICD-10), published by the WHO in 1992.

Intervention

Intervention can be a treatment, a change in practice or procedure, the introduction of a screening programme, etc.

Mean

The average value, calculated by adding together all the measurements and dividing by the number of measurements.

Median

The value on a scale that divides the distribution into two equal parts. Half the observations have a value less than or equal to the median, and half have a value greater than or equal to the median.

Meta-analysis

A statistical technique that summarises the results of several studies into a single estimate, giving more weight to results from larger studies.

Methodology

The methods and principles used in a piece of work. For example, authors of a systematic review will explain its methodology in terms of their search strategy, criteria for including trials, statistical methods used, etc.

Null hypothesis

This describes the outcome expected if the intervention group were no different from the control group. A statistical test examines whether an experimental result could have happened merely by chance and the treatment is really ineffective (null hypothesis is true).

Odds

Odds is the probability that an event will happen.

Odds ratio (OR)

This is the odds in the treatment group divided by the odds in the control group. It is one measure of the clinical effectiveness of a treatment. If it is equal to 1, then the effects of the treatment are no different from those of the control treatment. If we are looking for more of something (eg stopping smoking) and an intervention works, the OR will be greater than 1. If we are looking for less of something (eg death or disability) and the intervention works, the OR will be less than 1. The OR is statistically significant if the confidence interval around the OR does not include 1.

Outcome

The result of an intervention. Outcomes can be desirable, such as an improvement in the patient's condition or quality of life, or undesirable, such as side effects.

Population

This describes the people that researchers are interested in. Information about them might include age, gender, and state of health.

Prevalence

The number of cases of a disease (or other outcome of interest) in a defined population at a specified point in time, taken as a proportion of the total number of people in that population during that time.

Primary care

Family health services provided by a range of practitioners including family doctors, community nurses and other interests.

Prospective studies

Studies designed before any data are collected. A cohort study is a kind of prospective study.

p-value

The probability that the observed results in a study could have occurred by chance. The p-value can be any value between 0 and 1. 0 indicates that the results could not have happened by chance, while 1 shows that it is certain that they did. All studies have a p-value between these two extremes. A p-value of 0.05 indicates that there is only a 1 in 20 probability that the result happened by chance. Thus any p-value less than this is taken as a reasonably good indication that the result is statistically significant.

Randomisation

Subjects in a population are randomly allocated to groups, usually called treatment and control groups. Allocation of participants to groups is therefore determined by chance. In robust randomisation procedures all individuals have the same probability of being allocated either to the experimental or to the control groups.

Randomised controlled trial (RCT)

An RCT is a trial in which subjects are randomly assigned to two groups: one (the experimental group) receives the intervention that is being tested, and the other (the comparison group or control group) receives an alternative treatment. The results of the trial are assessed by comparing the outcomes in the different groups.

Random error

Random error or random variation refers to the differences in results that are due to chance rather than to one of the other variables being studied. Differences caused by random error cause results to be scattered randomly about the mean or best estimate.

Reliability

The process of establishing that data analysis and coding remains constant when reviewed at different times by the same researcher (stability) or another researcher (reproducibility).

Reproducible

Capable of being reproduced. Authors of research reports should describe their methods thoroughly so that others can try to reproduce their results.

Retrospective studies

Studies in which existing data, often generated for a different purpose, are reanalysed to explore a question of interest.

Review

Any summary of a particular topic.

Risk

Risk is used to describe the chance that something will happen. Researchers often use the word 'risk' to state the proportion of a group of patients in whom an event is observed.

Sensitivity

In a literature search, sensitivity is the likelihood of retrieving all relevant items. That is, a sensitive search is a broad search as it will also include a number of items that may not be relevant.

Standard deviation (SD)

The mean, median and mode are measures of central tendency and are useful for summarising a frequency distribution, but they do not include the spread of values. The SD measures the amount of scatter in results. Approximately two-thirds of the values will fall within 1 SD of the mean and 95% within 2 SD of the mean.

Statistical significance

A result that is very unlikely to have happened by chance is often described as statistically significant. Researchers often use statistical tests such as chi-squared and the probability value to check whether their results are statistically significant.

Surrogate (proxy) outcome measure

A surrogate outcome measure is an end point used instead of one that is usually more meaningful clinically but more difficult to measure practically. For example, bone mineral density is often used as a surrogate outcome measure for bone fracture in clinical trials of prophylactic treatments such as hormone replacement therapy.

Systematic error

Systematic error refers to consistent differences in results from the true value. Systematic error tends to be caused by some kind of bias. The two principal biases are selection bias and measurement bias.

Validity

Refers to the soundness or rigour of a study. A study is valid if the way it is designed and carried out means that the results are unbiased, ie it gives a 'true' estimate of clinical effectiveness.

List of seminar contributors

Dr John Bamford

Consultant Neurologist, St James's University Hospital, Leeds

Professor David Barer

Stroke Research Team, Institute for the Health of the Elderly, Queen Elizabeth Hospital, Newcastle (*Workshop Chair*)

Ms Anne Blackburn

Physiotherapist, Warwick Hospital, Warwick

Dr Ibrahim Bodagh

Staff Grade Physician, Southampton University Hospitals NHS Trust, Southampton General Hospital

Ms Jo Booth

Barnes Hospital, Cheshire

Ms Fiona Brockwell

Stroke Co-ordinator, Stoke Mandeville Hospital NHS Trust, Bucks

Ms Melanie Chapman

Research Fellow in Health Care Practice, University of Salford

Dr David Chappel

Lecturer in Public Health Medicine, School of Health Sciences, University of Newcastle, Newcastle upon Tyne

Ms Diane Cherry

Stroke Research Nurse, Leicester Royal Infirmary NHS Trust, Leicester Royal Infirmary

Ms Linda Christie

Stroke Co-ordinator, North Staffordshire Combined Healthcare NHS Trust, Bucknall Hospital, Stoke on Trent

Mr Robert Cleary

Director, Outcomes Development Programme, CASPE Research, King's Fund, London

Ms Jane Davies

Physiotherapist, Selly Oak Hospital, Birmingham

Ms Hazel Dickinson

Research Assistant, Fazakerley Hospital, Liverpool

Dr Christopher Durkin

Consultant Physician in Geriatric and General Medicine, Stoke Mandeville Hospital NHS Trust, Bucks

Ms Caroline Ellis-Hill

Research Occupational Therapist, University of Southampton

Ms Susan Fall

Research Co-ordinator, Stroke Research Team, Institute for the Health of the Elderly, Queen Elizabeth Hospital, Gateshead

Mr Andrew Georgiou

Research Associate, Outcomes Measurement, Clinical Effectiveness and Evaluation Unit, Royal College of Physicians, London *(Background paper)*

Dr Michael Goldacre

Director, Unit of Healthcare Epidemiology, University of Oxford *(Background paper)*

Dr Kizhakke Gopinathan

Staff Grade Physician, Warwick Hospital, Warwick

Ms Shelagh Gowing

Stroke Specialist Nurse, Heatherwood and Wexham Park Hospitals NHS Trust, Slough

Professor Walter Holland

Emeritus Professor of Public Health Medicine, London School of Economics and Political Science *(Workshop Chair)*

Ms Penny Irwin

Research Associate – Stroke, Clinical Effectiveness and Evaluation Unit, Royal College of Physicians, London *(Background paper)*

Ms Emma Jackson

Stroke Research Nurse, St James's University Hospital, Leeds

Dr Marcia Kelson

Senior Research Fellow, College of Health, London

Mr Michael Leathley

Stroke Research Co-ordinator, Aintree Hospitals NHS Trust, Liverpool

Dr Jonathan Mant

Senior Lecturer, University of Birmingham Medical School *(Background paper)*

Dr Peter Mayer

Consultant Physician (Geriatric Medicine), Selly Oak Hospital, Birmingham

Dr Peter W Overstall

Consultant in Geriatric Medicine, Hereford General Hospital, Hereford

Dr Michael Pearson

Director, Clinical Effectiveness and Evaluation Unit, Royal College of Physicians; Consultant Physician, Aintree Chest Centre, Fazakerley Hospital, Liverpool *(Chair)*

Dr Michael W Pearson

Consultant Physician, Battle Hospital, Reading

Ms Bridget Penhale

Lecturer in Social Work, University of Hull

Ms Sue Portlock

Stroke Co-ordinator, Selly Oak Hospital, Birmingham

Ms Mary Price

Occupational Therapist, Wexham Park Hospital, Slough

Ms Michelle Probert

Stroke Discharge Team, Hereford General Hospital, Hereford

Miss Stella Pronk

Senior Occupational Therapist, Southampton Hospital, Southampton

Dr Helen Roberts

Consultant in Geriatric Medicine, Southampton Hospital, Southampton

Dr Anthony Rudd

Consultant Physician, St. Thomas's Hospital, London *(Background paper)*

Ms Zoë Rutledge

National Stroke Audit Co-ordinator, Clinical Effectiveness and Evaluation Unit, Royal College of Physicians, London

Dr Anil Sharma

Consultant Physician, Fazakerley Hospital, Liverpool

Mrs Sandy Thompson

Research Associate – Lung Cancer, Clinical Effectiveness and Evaluation Unit, Royal College of Physicians, London

Mr Frazer Underwood

Key Worker, Stroke Research Team, Leicester Royal Infirmary

Dr Annelies Vreeburg

Bucknall Hospital, Stoke on Trent

Professor Derick Wade

Consultant in Neurological Disabilities, Rivermead Rehabilitation Centre, Oxford *(Workshop Chair)*

Bibliography

Aho K, Reunanen A, Aromaa A, Knekt P *et al*. Prevalence of stroke in Finland. *Stroke* 1986; **17**: 681–6.

Alexander MP. Stroke rehabilitation outcome: a potential use of predictive variables to establish levels of care. *Stroke* 1994; **25**: 128–34.

Anderson C. Baseline measures and outcome predictions. *Neuroepidemiology* 1994; **13**: 283–9.

Bamford J, Sandercock P, Warlow C, Gray M. Why are patients with acute stroke admitted to hospital? *Br Med J* 1986; **292**: 1369–72.

Bamford J, Sandercock P, Jones L, Warlow C. The natural history of lacunar infarction: the Oxfordshire Community Stroke Project. *Stroke* 1987; **18**: 545–51.

Bamford J, Sandercock P, Dennis M, Warlow C, *et al*. A prospective study of acute cerebrovascular disease in the community: the Oxfordshire Community Stroke Project. 1. Methodology, demography and incident cases of first-ever stroke. *J Neurol Neurosurg Psychiatry* 1988; **51**: 1373–80.

Bamford J, Sandercock P, Dennis M, Burn J, *et al*. A prospective study of acute cerebrovascular disease in the community: The Oxfordshire Community Stroke Project. 2. Incidence, case fatality rates and overall outcome at one year of cerebral infarction, primary intracerebral and subarachnoid haemorrhage. *J Neurol Neurosurg Psychiatry* 1990; **53**: 16–22.

Bamford J, Dennis M, Sandercock P, Burn J, *et al*. The frequency, causes and timing of death within 30 days of a first-ever stroke: the Oxfordshire Community Stroke Project. *J Neurol Neurosurg Psychiatry* 1990; **53**: 824–9.

Bamford J, Sandercock P, Dennis M, Warlow C. Classification and natural history of clinically identifiable subtypes of cerebral infarction. *Lancet* 1991; **337**: 1521–6.

Barer DH. Lower cranial motor function in unilateral vascular lesions of the cerebral hemisphere. *Br Med J* 1984; **289**: 1621–2.

Barer DH. Continence after stroke: useful predictor or goal of therapy? *Age Ageing* 1989; **18**:183–91.

Barer DH. The natural history and functional consequences of dysphagia after hemispheric stroke. *J Neurol Neurosurg Psychiatry* 1989; **52**: 236–41.

Barer DH. Stroke in Nottingham: the burden of nursing care and possible implications for the future. *Clin Rehabil* 1991; **5**: 103–10.

Barer D, Murphy J. Scaling the Barthel: a 10-point hierarchical version of the activities of daily living index for use with stroke patients. *Clin Rehabil* 1993; **7**: 221–7.

Beech R, Withey C, Morris R. Understanding variations in lengths of stay between hospitals for fractured neck of femur patients and the potential consequences of reduced stay targets. *J Public Health Med* 1995; **17**: 77–84.

Benbow SJ, Watkins C, Sangster G, Ellul J, *et al*. The availability and reliability of information on the pre-morbid functional status of stroke patients in hospital. *Clin Rehabil* 1994; **8**: 281–5.

Bonita R. Epidemiology of stroke. *Lancet* 1992; **339**: 342–4.

Bonita R, Beaglehole R, North JDK. Event, incidence and case fatality rates of cerebrovascular disease in Auckland, New Zealand. *Am J Epidemiol* 1984; **120**: 236–43.

Bonita R, Thompson S. Subarachnoid haemorrhage: epidemiology, diagnosis, management and outcome. *Stroke* 1985; **16**: 591–4.

Bonita R, Ford MA, Stewart AW. Predicting survival after stroke: a three-year follow-up. *Stroke* 1988; **19**: 669–73.

Bonita R, Broad JB, Beaglehole R. Changes in stroke incidence and case-fatality in Auckland, New Zealand 1981–91. *Lancet* 1993; **342**: 1470–3.

Bounds JV, Wiebers DO, Whisant JP, Okazaki H. Mechanisms and timing of deaths from cerebral infarction. *Stroke* 1981; **12**: 474–7.

Bunn F. The needs of families and carers of stroke patients. In: Wolfe C, Rudd A, Beech R (eds) *Stroke services and research.* Stroke Association, 1996.

Christie D. Prevalence of stroke and its sequelae. *Med J Aust* 1981; **2**: 182–4.

Clark M, Watts S. The incidence of pressure sores within a National Health Service trust hospital during 1991. *J Adv Nurs* 1994; **20**: 33–6.

Clinical Standards Advisory Group. Report on clinical effectiveness using stroke care as an example. London: The Stationary Office, 1998.

Davenport RJ, Dennis MS, Warlow CP. Effect of correcting outcome data for case mix: an example from stroke medicine. *Br Med J* 1996; **312**: 1503–5.

Dennis MS, Burn JPS, Sandercock AG, Bamford JM, *et al.* Long-term survival after first-ever stroke: the Oxfordshire Community Stroke Project. *Stroke* 1993; **24**: 796–800.

Department of Health. *A first class service: quality in the new NHS.* London: HMSO, 1998.

Department of Health. *Hospital Episode Statistics.* Volumes 1 and 2. Financial year 1993–94. Leeds: Department of Health, 1995.

Department of Health. *Hospital Episode Statistics.* Volumes 1 and 2. England. Financial year 1994–95. Leeds: Department of Health, 1996.

Department of Health. *Public Health Common Data Set* 1995. Institute of Public Health, University of Surrey, 1996.

Department of Health. *The new NHS – modern dependable: a national framework for assessing performance.* London: Department of Health, 1997.

Department of Health. Our healthier nation: a contract for health. London: HMSO, 1998.

Dyken ML. Natural history of ischaemic stroke in cerebrovascular disease. In: Harrison MJG, Dyken ML (eds). Butterworth international medical reviews: *Neurology,* edition 3. London: Butterworth, 1983: 139–70.

Ebrahim S, Barer D, Nouri F. An audit of follow-up services for stroke patients after discharge from hospital. *Int Disabil Stud* 1987; **9**: 103–5.

Effective Health Care. *The prevention and treatment of pressure sores.* Nuffield Institute for Health, University of Leeds; NHS Centre for Reviews and Dissemination, University of York, 1995.

Ellul J, Watkins C, Barer D. Estimating total Barthel scores from just three items: the European Stroke Database minimum dataset for assessing functional status at discharge from hospital. In press.

Garraway W, Whisnant J, Drury I. The continuing decline in the incidence of stroke. *Mayo Clin Proc* 1983; **58**: 520–3.

Gladman J, Albazzaz M, Barer D. A survey of survivors of acute stroke discharged from hospitals to private nursing homes in Nottingham. *Health Trends* 1991; **23**: 158–60.

Glass TA, Matchar DB, Belyea M, Feussner JR. Impact of social support on outcome in stroke. *Stroke* 1993; **24**: 64–70.

Goldstein LB, Matchar DB. Clinical assessement of stroke. *J Am Med Assoc* 1994; **271**:1114–20.

Gompertz P, Pound P, Ebrahim S. The reliability of stroke outcome measures. *Clin Rehabil* 1993; **7**: 290–6.

Gordon C, Langton-Hewer RL, Wade DT. Dysphagia in acute stroke. *Br Med J* 1987; **295**: 411–4.

Green J, Wintfeld N. Report cards on cardiac surgeons: assessing New York State's approach. *N Engl J Med* 1995; **332**: 1229–32.

Hatona S. Experience from a multicenter stroke register: a preliminary report. *Bull WHO* 1976; 54: 541–53.

Healey F. Using incidence data to improve risk assessment. *J Tissue Viability* 1996; **6**: 3–9.

Herman B, Leyten ACM, Van Luijk JH, Frenken CWGM, *et al.* Epidemiology of stroke in Tilburg, The Netherlands. The population-based stroke incidence register. 2. Incidence, initial clinical picture and medical care, and three-week case fatality. *Stroke* 1982; **13**: 629–34.

Hillman M, Geddes JML, Tennant A, Chamberlain MA. Benefits and services: stroke survivors living in the community. Stroke Association Annual Scientific Conference, London, 1995.

Iezzoni LI, Ash AS, Schwartz M, Daley J *et al.* Predicting who dies depends on how severity is measured: implications for evaluating patient outcomes. *Ann Intern Med* 1995; **123**: 763–70.

Irwin P, Rudd A. Casemix and process indicators of outcome in stroke: the Royal College of Physicians minimum data set for stroke. *J R Coll Physicians Lond* 1998; **32**: 442–4.

Kelly-Hayes M, Wolf PA, Kannel WB, Sytkowski P *et al.* Factors influencing survival and need for institutionalisation following stroke: The Framingham study. *Arch Phys Med Rehabil* 1988; **69**: 415–8.

King's Fund Consensus Statement. Treatment of stroke. *Br Med J* 1988; **297**: 126–8.

Kojima S, Omura T, Wakamatsu W, Kisni M, *et al.* Prognosis and disability of stroke patients after 5 years in Akita, Japan. *Stroke* 1990; **21**: 72–7.

Last JM. *A Dictionary of Epidemiology* (second edition). London: Oxford University Press, 1988.

Legh-Smith J, Wade DT, Langton-Hewer R. Services for stroke patients one year after stroke. *J Epidemiol Community Health* 1986; **40**: 161–5.

Lincoln NB, Jackson JM, Edmans JA, Walker MF *et al.* The accuracy of prediction about progress of patients on a stroke unit. *J Neurol Neurosurg Psychiatry* 1990; **53**: 972–75.

Lindley RI, Amayo EO, Marshall J, Sandercock PAG, *et al.* Hospital services for patients with acute stroke in the United Kingdom: the Stroke Association survey of consultant opinion. *Age Ageing* 1995; **24**: 525–32.

Long A. Assessing health and social outcomes. In: Popay J, Williams G. *Researching the people's health.* London: Routledge, 1994.

Malmgren R, Bamford J, Warlow C, Sandercock P. Geographical and secular trends in stroke incidence. *Lancet* 1987; **ii**: 1196–2000.

Malmgren R, Bamford J, Warlow C, Sandercock P, *et al.* Projecting the number of patients with first-ever strokes and patients newly handicapped by stroke in England and Wales. *Br Med J* 1989; **298**: 656–60.

Mant J, Mant F, Winner S. How good is routine information? Validation of coding for acute stroke in Oxford hospitals. *Health Trends* 1997/98; **28**: 96–9.

Martin J, White A, Meltzer H. *Office of Population Censuses and Surveys. Disabled adults: services, transport and employment (report 4, Disability in Greater Britain).* London: HMSO, 1989.

Mayor S. *How to reduce your risk of stroke.* London: Stroke Association, 1997.

Nakayama H, Jogensen HS, Raaschou HO, Olsen TS. The influence of age on stroke outcome: the Copenhagen Study. *Stroke* 1994; **25**: 808–13.

National Pressure Ulcer Advisory Panel. Pressure ulcers prevalence, cost and risk assessment. Consensus development statement. *Care – Decubitus* 1989; **2**: 24–8.

NHS Centre for Reviews and Dissemination, University of York. *Effective health care.* Vol 2, no 1,1995.

NHS Management Executive. *Priorities and planning guidance 1994–95. EL(93)54.* Leeds: Department of Health, 1993.

Odderson IR, McKenna BS. A model for management of patients with stroke during the acute phase, outcome and economic implications. *Stroke* 1993; **24**: 1823–7.

Odderson IR, Keaton JC, McKenna BS. Swallow management in patients on an acute stroke pathway : quality is cost effective. *Arch Phys Med Rehabil* 1995; **76**: 1130–3.

Office of National Statistics. Series DH 2, no 24 *Mortality statistics: causes. England & Wales 1997.* London: HMSO, 1998.

Office of Population Censuses and Surveys. *Morbidity statistics from general practice 1991–1992.* London: HMSO, 1995.

O'Mahony PG, Dobson R, Rodgers H, James OFW, *et al.* Validation of a population screening questionnaire to assess prevalence of stroke. *Stroke* 1995; **26**: 1334–7.

Oxfordshire Community Stroke Project. Incidence of stroke in Oxfordshire: first year's experience of a community stroke register. *Br Med J* 1983; **287**: 713–7.

Patrick DL, Erickson P. *Health status and health policy.* Oxford: Oxford University Press, 1993.

Riddell JA. Out-of-hours visits in a group practice. *Br Med J* 1980; **i**: 1518–20.

Royal College of Physicians of London. *Stroke – towards better management.* London: RCP, 1989.

Rudd A, Goldacre M, Amess M, Fletcher J, *et al.* (eds). *Health outcome indicators: Stroke. Report of a working group to the Department of Health.* Oxford: National Centre for Health Outcomes Development, 1999.

Sacco RL, Wolf PA, Kannel WB, McNamara PM. Survival and recurrence following stroke: the Framingham Study. *Stroke* 1982; **13**: 290–5.

Sandercock PAG. *The Oxfordshire Community Stroke Project and its application to stroke prevention.* MD Thesis, University of Oxford, 1984.

Sarti C, Tuomilehto J, Salomaa V, Sivenius J, *et al.* Epidemiology of subarachnoid haemorrhage in Finland from 1983 to 1985. *Stroke* 1991; **22**: 848–53.

Scmidt EV, Smirnov VE, Ryabova VS. Results of the seven-year prospective study of stroke patients. *Stroke* 1988; **19**: 942–9.

Scottish Intercollegiate Guidelines Network. *A National Clinical Guideline recommended for use in Scotland by the Scottish Intercollegiate Guideline Network (SIGN).* III. Identification and management of dysphagia. Edinburgh: SIGN, 1997.

Smith DM. Pressure ulcers in the nursing home. *Ann Intern Med* 1995; **123**: 433–42.

Smith I. Waterlow/Norton scoring system: a ward view. *CARE–Science and Practice* 1989; **7**: 93–5.

Sorensen PS, Boysen G, Jensen G, Schnohr P. Prevalence of stroke in a district of Copenhagen: the Copenhagen City Heart Study. *Acta Neurol Scand* 1982; **66**: 68–81.

Sotaniemi KA, Pyhtinen J, Myllya VV. Correlation of clinical and computed tomographic findings in stroke patients. *Stroke* 1990; **21**: 1562–6.

Stewart JA, Dundas R, Howard RS, Rudd AG, *et al.* Ethnic differences in stroke incidence: a prospective study using a stroke register. *Br Med J* 1999; **318**: 967–71.

Stone SP, Ali B, Auberleek I, Thompsell A, *et al.* The Barthel Index in clinical practice: use on a rehabilitation ward for elderly people. *J R Coll Physicians Lond* 1994; **28**: 419–23.

Stroke Unit Trialists' Collaboration. A systematic review of specialist multi-disciplinary team (stroke unit) care for stroke in patients. In: *The Cochrane Database of Systematic Reviews: Stroke Module* (ed. Warlow C, Van Gijn J, Sandercock P). BMJ Publishing Group, 1995.

Stroke Unit Trialists' Collaboration. Collaborative systematic review of the randomised trials of organised inpatient (stroke unit) care after stroke. *Br Med J* 1997; **314**: 1151–9.

Stroke Unit Trialists' Collaboration. How do stroke units improve patient outcomes? A collaborative systematic review of the randomised trials. *Stroke* 1997; **28**: 2139–44.

Sudlow CL, Warlow CP. Comparable studies of the incidence of stroke and its pathological types: results from the International Stroke Incidence Collaboration. *Stroke* 1997; **28**: 491–9.

Terent A. Survival after stroke and transient ischaemic attacks during the 1970s and 1980s. *Stroke* 1989; **20**: 1320–6.

Thorvaldsen P, Asplund K, Kuutasmaa K, Rajaknagas AM, *et al*. Stroke incidence, case fatality, and mortality in the WHO MONICA project. *Stroke* 1995; **26**: 361–7.

Underwood F, Parker J. Developing and evaluating an acute stroke care pathway through action research. *Nurse Researcher* 1999; **1**(2): 27–38.

Wade DT, Langton-Hewer R, Wood VA. Stroke: influence of patient's sex and side of weakness on outcome. *Arch Phys Med Rehabil* 1984; **65**; 513–6.

Wade DT, Langton-Hewer R, Skilbeck CE, Bainton D, *et al*. Controlled trial of home care service for acute stroke patients. *Lancet* 1985; **ii**: 323–6.

Wade DT, Langton-Hewer R. Outcome after an acute stroke: urinary incontinence and loss of consciousness compared in 532 patients. *Q J Med* 1985; **221**: 347–52.

Wade DT, Parker V, Langton-Hewer R. Memory disturbance after stroke; frequency and associated losses. *Int Rehabil Med* 1986; **8**: 60–4.

Wade DT, Langton-Hewer R. Functional abilities after stroke: measurement, natural history and prognosis. *J Neurol Neurosurg Psychiatry* 1987; **50**: 177–82.

Wade DT, Skilbeck CE, Langton-Hewer R. Selected cognitive losses after stroke. Frequency, recovery and prognostic importance. *Int Disabil Stud* 1989; **11**: 34–9.

Wade DT. Stroke (acute cerebrovascular disease). In: Stevens A, Raftery J (eds). *Health care needs assessment: the epidemiology based needs assessment reviews*. Oxford: Radcliffe Medical Press, 1994.

Ween JE, Alexander MP, D'Esposito M, Roberts M. Factors predictive of stroke outcome in a rehabilitation setting. *Neurology* 1996; **47**: 388–92.

Ween JE, Alexander MP, D'Esposito M, Roberts M. Incontinence after stroke in a rehabilitation setting: outcome associations and predictive factors. *Neurology* 1996; **47**(2): 388–92.

Ween JE, Alexander MP, D'Esposito M, Roberts M. Incontinence after stroke in a rehabilitation setting: outcome associations and predictive factors. *Neurology* 1996; **47**(3): 659–63.

West Lambeth Health Authority. Setting district stroke standards and objectives: a report of the West Lambeth Health Authority Stroke Steering Group. *J R Coll Physicians* Lond 1992; **26**: 172–6.

Westling B, Norving M, Thorngren M. Survival following stroke: a prospective population based study of 438 hospitalised cases with prediction according to subtype, severity and age. *Acta Neurol Scand* 1990; **81**: 457–63.

Wilkinson PR, Wolfe CDA, Warburton FG, Rudd AG, *et al*. A long-term follow-up of stroke patients. *Stroke* 1997; **28**: 507–512.

Wolfe CD, Burney PGJ. Is stroke mortality on the decline in England? *Am J Epidemiol* 1992; **136**: 558–65.

Wolfe CD, Taub NA, Woodrow J, Richardson E, *et al*. Does the incidence, severity or case fatality of stroke vary in southern England? *J Epidemiol Community Health* 1993; **47**: 139–43.

Wolfe CD, Taub NA, Woodrow J, Richardson E, *et al*. Patterns of acute stroke care in three districts of southern England. *J Epidemiol Community Health* 1993; **47**: 144–8.

Wolfe CD, Beech R, Ratcliffe M, Rudd AG. Stroke care in Europe: can we learn lessons from the different ways stroke is managed in different countries? *J R Soc Health* 1995; **115**: 143–7.

Wolfe CD, Taub NA, Bryan S, Beech R, *et al*. Variations in the incidence, management and outcome of stroke in residents under the age of 75 in two health districts of southern England. *J Public Health Med* 1995; **17**: 411–8.

Wolfe CD, Tilling K, Beech R, Rudd AG *et al.* Variations in case fatality and dependency from stroke in western and central Europe. The European BIOMED Study of Stroke Care Group. *Stroke* 1999; **30**: 350–6.

World Health Organization. *International classification of disease*, 9th revision, volume 1. London: HMSO, 1977.

World Health Organization. *The international classification of impairments, disabilities and handicaps.* Geneva: WHO, 1980.